LEADERSHIP:

ACHIEVING LIFE-CHANGING SUCCESS FROM WITHIN

By Sergeant Major Alford L. McMichael
USMC, Ret.

THRESHOLD
EDITIONS

New York London Toronto Sydney

Threshold Editions
A Division of Simon & Schuster, Inc.
1230 Avenue of the Americas
New York, NY 10020

First Threshold Editions hardcover edition May 2008

THRESHOLD EDITIONS and colophon are trademarks of Simon & Schuster, Inc.

For information about special discounts for bulk purchases,
please contact Simon & Schuster Special Sales at
1-800-456-6798 or business©simonandschuster.com.

Designed by Jamie Kerner-Scott

Manufactured in the United States of America

10 9 8 7 6 5 4 3 2 1

ISBN-13: 978-1-4165-6228-3
ISBN-10:   1-4165-6228-1

Acknowledgments

Mark Vancil—Thanks for having the right touch and feeling to bring my voice to this book, and for that I will always be grateful. Without your expertise this project wouldn't have been possible.

The United States Marines—for giving me the opportunity to use my life as an expression of my passion, which is loving people. And to the thousands of men and women around the world who, like myself, raised our hands to support and defend this great nation.

General James L. Jones—Thank you for not only making a difference in my life but for the support you have given me and my family from day one. This book is all about what you give the people of this nation every day, and that is great leadership.

My family—I want to thank my sisters and brothers for giving me the many examples that made it possible for me to write this book. I will always be thankful for the words of our grandmother Ida, who taught us "if one had, we all had."

Portia Blunt—for being on top of this project from day one and ensuring it was about leadership with passion. Your enthusism and excitement is contagious. You have always found new ways to bring love to this family. First with the best son-in-law anyone could wish for, Darren Blunt, and then Andrew, my grandson, and the reason leadership remains so important in my life.

ACKNOWLEDGMENTS

Simon and Schuster, Inc.—for allowing me to articulate the art of leadership in my own words. It has been an honor to work on this project with you.

And most of all to Rita McMichael, my wife. There are not enough words to thank you for the amazing life you have provided for me during the past thirty years. You helped me connect my childhood life and my adult life in a way only a person with a heart full of love, kindness, and respect could make happen.

Contents

Foreword

MARINE CORPS COMMANDANTS GET to do a lot of interesting things while they are in office. However, one of the most important tasks a commandant has to perform actually takes place before he/she takes office: the designation of the next Sergeant Major of the Marine Corps. The outgoing commandant convenes an informal search committee to identify the top four or five candidates from among all active-duty sergeants major. The commandant-designee then interviews each candidate and selects from among them the next Sergeant Major of the entire Corps.

The best decision I made as commandant happened before I even took office. It was the selection of Alford McMichael (and his wife Rita!) to become the 14th Sergeant Major of the Marine Corps.

Sergeant Major McMichael and I had never served together and did not know each other, but it was very quickly apparent from our initial meeting that this was the Marine I wanted at my side for the important work that needed to be done from 1999–2003. His performance of duty is still, in my view, the standard by which most others will be judged in the future.

What I admire about him is his selflessness, professionalism, and his compassion. For him, being a Marine has not been a job but a privileged calling; and he has lived each day of his remarkable career as though it might be his last, to be savored and treasured for eternity. He is fortunate in that he also looks like a Marine Corps recruiting poster, "right out of Central Casting" as Marines say in describing a Marine who is "squared away." Forget the fact that he was the first black Marine to be appointed to this post; he took on the role so immediately that all Marines quickly came to the conclusion that this was a leader to be admired, emulated, and followed . . . and that's exactly what all Marines did.

Sergeant Major McMichael will tell you that being fair and consistent are two of the most important attributes to being a good leader. He will tell you that deflecting credit toward others is another. But he also will be equally quick to point out that holding high the standard of achievement is also very important.

One of Sergeant Major McMichael's most satisfying moments came when the Marine Corps took the decision to rebuild all of our on-base housing units, starting with those for the most junior enlisted Marines. He figured importantly in this issue, just as he did in the decision to modernize the Marine Corps "utility" field uniform and combat boots in such a way that it saved out of pocket expenses for the Marines, yet gave them much better products. Not surprisingly the other services quickly followed suit in imitation.

Sergeant Major McMichael could have retired in the summer of 2003, something that each of his 13 predecessors did at the end of their tours. I asked him to take on another unique assignment in becoming the very first sergeant major of the North Atlantic Treaty Organization's (NATO) Allied Command Operations in Mons, Belgium. He and his wife, Rita, accepted and he set about bringing his unique skills to the world's most important alliance, a position that required exceptional political and military skills. Suffice it to say that in a short time he persuaded several nations to create Noncommissioned Officer Corps, where there had been none before, in their regular military establishments.

Leadership is the art of influencing people to do things they might not otherwise do in achieving desired goals. The more senior the leader, the more difficult the challenge. But not so for Al McMichael. The more senior he became, the more he came into his comfort zone because results never were about him—they were always about others.

Read this book carefully. It was written by a man who was raised on a dead-end street in Hot Springs, Arkansas. He had a mother, nine brothers and sisters and a grandmother, who never let him believe that a dead-end street meant a dead-end life. His family conferred upon him a gift—the motivation to rise to his full potential. He became a leader; he became a sergeant major of Marines, and a sergeant major of the operational troops of NATO.

We are all the better for his success, and we owe both him and Rita a debt of thanks for sharing a remarkable story with us.

—GENERAL JAMES L. JONES, USMC, RET.

Introduction

I GRADUATED FROM THE GREATEST leadership institution on earth with the highest honors. All it took me was thirty-six years of study, home and abroad.

Whatever my mother, Miss Rosa, my grandmother Miss Ida, and two older sisters, Ida Mae and Ruby, failed to teach me about leadership, the United States Marine Corps covered many times over. This is a book of principles and lessons, some of them learned at home in times far different than these. Others were developed, honed, and put into practice all over the world in a variety of leadership positions including the fourteenth Sergeant Major of the Marine Corps.

The fabric that binds all these ideas together was woven at the dinner table in a small house on Helm Street in Hot Springs, Arkansas, in the 1950s and '60s with my grandmother at the head and my mother in the kitchen. These are values and fundamental concepts about compassion, commitment, honesty, integrity, and good old-fashioned discipline. No one can lead well without first truly caring. The test often comes when the only eyes in the room are ours, with no one else there to measure, applaud, decry, or defend our actions.

The book is divided into ten principles, each one explained through anecdote and example.

Walk the Walk provides a map of the road that led me to follow my brother, Sherman, into the Marine Corps. What started out as a short-term escape turned into a long, unique military career.

Practice Dinner Table Values lays out the propositions driven into me growing up by two of the strongest women I have ever known inside or outside of the military. Not even the Marine Corps could have created the lessons in functional leadership taught day after day in words and actions throughout my childhood.

Impress Yourself First is an idea I learned from my grandmother's flawless example. Though she worked as a domestic and cleaned a classroom on the fourth floor of Hot Springs High School, Ida never felt beneath any person for even a day in her life. She set her standards high and lived her long life by them.

Rely on Intelligence over Emotion is the story of my experiences growing up in Hot Springs, Arkansas, as the Civil Rights movement rolled through the country and nearly unhinged parts of the south. It also covers my first introduction to racial extremes in the Marine Corps as the Vietnam War came to a close.

Prepare So You Can Prosper speaks to the hallmark of my career. Even before I knew what I was doing, I built systems and processes to navigate life. I knew instinctively the advantages and freedom that thorough preparation brought to my life.

Lead from the Heart is the application of compassion even in the highly charged world of the United States military. Sometimes issues of courage and honor are defined by the decisions we make when the written rules don't match the circumstances.

Rebuild What You Tear Down has universal application across age groups, businesses, and personal interactions of all kinds. The value of a human being is not diminished by any one single flaw, any more than a $100 bill is less valuable once it is no longer brand-new.

Give Power to Your People deals with the seemingly paradoxical notion that to enhance prospects for yourself and the organization often means a release to others of the very power most people think defines their strength.

Expect Excellence shows how the difference between good and great is often far less than it appears. Great leaders never settle for good when excellence is possible.

Foster Functional Leadership explores the practical application of these principles in real-life situations from high-level leadership positions around the world.

The final chapter, *Find Your Compass,* focuses on the difference old-fashioned leadership can make today both globally—and on an individual and community level.

Good leadership demands action. It entails developing insight into human nature, an inherent respect for those under our command, and plain hard work. Whether in full view of the culture, or the quiet of our own homes, the chance to lead well is there for all those who choose to do so.

My hope is that this book will provide an inside view into one man's journey through the halls of the greatest leadership-training program in the world. And that from my personal experience, others will learn some of the principles of strong leadership that I discovered along the way and put them into practice.

LEADERSHIP:

ACHIEVING LIFE-CHANGING SUCCESS FROM WITHIN

1

Walk the Walk:
The Lost Art of Leadership

THE BLACK-AND-WHITE TELEVISION SAT on top of a tall, black oak table just inside the front door and to the right. The one-story house had brown, faux brick siding and a porch that wrapped around the front. In the shadow of the Great Depression, my grandfather paid $800, a fortune at the time, for house No. 9 on Helm Street in Hot Springs, Arkansas, in the early 1930s. He was tagged with a thirty-year mortgage and monthly payments of three dollars.

I was born on February 24, 1952, and until I was five years old, Helm Street was a dirt road. Our plumbing was outdoors. The kitchen sink was simply a bucket where dishes were washed. The icebox was just that: a box where we put the ice from the ice house around the corner. The living room couldn't have been more appropriately named because that's where we lived.

Every day started in that room. It was the last stop before everyone left for school. My mother stood near the door, checked our hair, and made sure we had lunch money, our books, and all our homework. It was like a military inspection. We'd fall in, go through guard mount, and march out the door in an order determined by age, oldest to youngest. And every night ended there with us all in front of the boulder-like, twenty-four-inch Zenith television in its black-framed box.

But in 1969, that room and the television were my connection to a world beyond my imagination and to my only brother who had left home the year before. Named after our grandfather, Sherman was eighteen months older and just a grade ahead of me in school. Our lives had been intertwined to a degree unusual for even the closest of siblings. We were the men of a house dominated by women, a mother and grandmother, followed by two older sisters, ten of us children in all, and not even a photograph of a father.

Our family raised a large amount of the food we ate, my siblings and I hauling hundred-pound bags of feed to the backyard where we kept all the animals—a cow, chickens, rabbits, geese, and goats. By the time we kids were in middle school, there wasn't a teacher anywhere who could tell us more about the cycle of life in animals or the mating processes and patterns of rabbits. We helped our grandmother, Ida, grow most of the vegetables we ate, and we executed the commands of our mother, Miss Rosa, around the house.

By the time Sherman, who was then seventeen, told me he was going to drop out of our high school following his junior year, the dark clouds of a culture in transition had started to slowly edge into Hot Springs.

A gambling and entertainment mecca that rivaled Las Vegas just a decade earlier, Hot Springs was changing. Two groups with different agendas but a common cause—Baptists and gambling operatives from Nevada—worked hard to close down the casinos that had effectively kept Hot Springs in a time warp. Although the Civil Rights Act of

1964 allowed all African-Americans the right to enter theaters from the main street and go through the front doors of restaurants to order food, the racial and political tension rising from the streets of Chicago, New York, and Los Angeles were of a nature and intensity beyond anything we experienced in our home town.

Still, it was amid both the pain of assassination—first Dr. Martin Luther King's on April 4, 1968, then Robert Kennedy's on June 5, 1968—and the political turmoil in Chicago that Sherman chose a road that forever took him out of Hot Springs and into a conflicted and rapidly changing world.

He had been a cornerback on the last football team at Langston, the city's all-black high school. That fall, 1968, Langston and Hot Springs High, where former president Bill Clinton attended, were to be integrated at a new facility outside of town. The new school would be called Hot Springs High School. Langston would cease to exist, becoming instead a middle school.

"I'm not going to that school," Sherman said. "I'm not doing that. I grew up at Langston High. I'm done with school."

I looked at my brother. The words didn't match the person I had known all my life. How could anyone just stop going to school?

"How can you not go to school?" I asked. "How could that thought even enter your mind?"

In those days, you could drop out of high school and join the United States Marine Corps. That's exactly what Sherman did in the summer before his senior year.

On August 21, 1968, a Marine became the first African-American soldier awarded the Congressional Medal of Honor. A day later, as street clashes between demonstrators and police brought chaos to the Democratic National Convention, I started going to school with white people for the first time, and my brother prepared for war.

For all the changes I was going through, Sherman's transformation would be of a whole other magnitude.

When Sherman returned home from basic training four months later, he had muscles in places I had never seen muscles before. He had become a daredevil, fearless. But I still couldn't understand anything about why he chose the path he did. Why would he want to leave something so good, the life we had together as brothers in a family that had defined our entire lives?

I remember going to school one day when my brother was home on leave, and a kid telling me Sherman had been in a fight at a club the night before.

"Man, he hit this guy with one punch," said the boy, "and that guy went straight down to the floor."

My brother?

When Sherman left for Vietnam, I struggled to process that reality. Not even integration had as much impact on me as my brother going off to war all the way on the other side of the world. I thought about him all the time. I wrote him letters. I told him about my car, my girlfriend, what was happening at school and around town. Every night I prayed he'd be safe.

I understand now what parents and loved ones go through when their sons, daughters, husbands, and wives are in harm's way.

I was a seventeen-year-old kid looking up into the heavens and praying for the good Lord to watch over my brother. Every night I made sure I was home with a seat in front of that television in our living room to watch Walter Cronkite on the *CBS Evening News*. It was as if I needed to see that Vietnam footage to make sense of the path my brother had chosen.

I remember thinking back then, *Isn't the military for men? Don't you have to be a grown man to be a soldier?* My brother was a boy, just like me. Men looked like those fathers down the street heading off to the Reynold's Aluminum plant with their lunch boxes. Even with all those new muscles, to me, Sherman was still just a boy.

I'd swear that I caught a glimpse of him in the background of one of those Dan Rather reports, or in the film clip that went with the day's war story.

I know now that I never did see him.

Later on, when he came home briefly after thirteen months in Vietnam with a Purple Heart for having been wounded and other combat commendations on his chest, I knew he was no longer a boy. And to one degree or another, neither was I.

I remember when we first found out from the Marines that he had been wounded. There were no computers, cell phones, or phone cards at the time as a way for him to get in touch. We had no idea if he would make it back home, and if he did, how or when he would arrive.

When we finally got word that summer, I went to pick him up at the Little Rock bus terminal. I remember being proud to drive him around, though I still couldn't understand how he could tell grown men what to do. He had left as a private first class and now he was a corporal. He came home from the war with amazing stories of places and people, life and death. And he was listening to Jimi Hendrix, Janis Joplin, and all kinds of music that was as new and foreign to me as the war itself.

I still had no desire to follow Sherman into the military, much less the Marine Corps. But as my own graduation neared, I also knew I couldn't stay at home if I was going to grow into the man I wanted to become. I didn't know exactly what that looked like at the time, but I knew it didn't look anything like Hot Springs, Arkansas.

The Marine Corps recruiter pulled me over one day as I sat on the fence trying to decide what to do. *I'll put in my time,* I thought. *Then I'll head off to college.*

"You'll never make it in the Marines," Sherman told me when he found out my intentions.

But I enlisted in the United States Marine Corps anyway and arrived at the recruit depot in San Diego on August 27, 1970. It was two months after U.S. ground forces were pulled out of Cambodia, almost three weeks to the day before Jimi Hendrix died of a barbiturates overdose in London, and a little more than a month before Janis Joplin was found dead of a heroin overdose in Los Angeles.

In October, President Richard Nixon announced that as many as 40,000 troops were to be sent home from Vietnam. I had been given orders to be part of a Christmas replacement. We had gone through the battalion staging process, which was the last phase of training before the flight to Southeast Asia.

By December, the world was continuing to twist and turn. The United Nations General Assembly voted to support the isolation of South Africa over apartheid. Later, the north tower of the World Trade Center would become the tallest building in the world.

Then, as I prepared for Vietnam, my orders changed to Hawaii. Apparently so many Marines had been lost to drugs and other problems in Hawaii that we were diverted there to fill in.

I arrived as a PFC—private first class—one automatic promotion above private. Suddenly it was as if my training was over. I was made part of a unit, and I would perform every minute of every day for the next two years. This was the "spit and polish" Marine Corps everyone knows from the movies.

At the time the nation was still at war.

So were the officers in Hawaii.

No breaks, excuses, not even an inch of latitude were allowed. Perfection was the only standard. Anything else was failure.

It didn't take me long to appreciate the benefits of the Marine Corps' rigid structure. All you had to do was follow orders exactly as they were delivered. No freelancing, no second-guessing.

Sherman and I had grown up in a house run exactly the same way by two exceptionally strong women. My mother, Miss Rosa, operated as the drill sergeant while my grandmother, Ida, was the four-star general in charge. I became a very good Marine because the role was very clear to me.

What I didn't know was that Sherman had found his way to Hawaii as well. After Vietnam, my brother was stationed at Quantico, the Marine base in Virginia. When the Marine Corps asked him to reenlist, Sherman had the ability to choose his next duty station. As a decorated combat veteran, he took orders to Hawaii.

As I was processing in after arriving in Oahu, the first sergeant asked me if I had any relatives in the Marines Corps.

"Yes, sir," I said. "I have a brother."

"What's his name?"

"McMichael, sir."

Sherman's first name never even crossed my mind. After nearly six months of mind-shaping training, I had truly become a Marine.

THE MARINE CORPS WORKS its people hard physically, but even harder mentally. No way can a person go through a complete cycle of recruit training and have the same civilian mind-set he or she had the first day they walked off the bus. We are taught to think like Marines, and among other things that means nothing is impossible. If you are tired at three miles, then you are conditioned to believe that you have five more miles in you.

I had been taught how to reach down into places inside me and find whatever I needed—even when I knew there was nothing else to get. There were times when I could hear the voice of my grandmother, a woman who could outwork any man on his best day, saying, "When you think it's good, make it better. When it seems impossible, make it a possibility."

The next thing I knew, my brother walked down the stairs. He was the duty NCO, which means he was responsible for the daily operation of the command in the absence of the commanding officer. Noncommissioned officers come from the ranks of enlisted Marines, whereas commissioned officers come from a college Reserve Officer Training Corps (ROTC) program, Officer Candidate School, and the Naval Academy.

I hadn't seen him in a long while. And yet, there he was. This was the same guy who used to sleep in bed with me, the same guy who used to eat my food, wear my clothes, and take my things to make me cry.

But this was the Marine Corps. His uniform was Marine perfect. He had spent more than a year fighting a war in jungles, and he had felt the sting of shrapnel entering his body. He had medals, experience, and rank. We might as well have been strangers.

"I'm glad you are here," he said matter-of-factly.

Then I was immediately transferred to the Naval Communication Station fifty miles away in Wahiawa at the far end of Whitmore Village, down a road that ran through Dole pineapple fields. We belonged to the same command, but I very quickly found out that's about all we still had in common.

When I finally figured out the phone system, the first call I made was to Sherman.

"Hey, how are you doing?" I said when my brother answered the phone.

"Who is this?"

"It's me, Al."

"Are you an NCO?"

"No."

"If you're not an NCO, then I don't talk to you."

He hung up the phone.

In a little over those two years, my brother had been around the world. At that moment I wasn't sure whether he had come back. But I thought, *Okay, I'll show him. If he's good enough to be a sergeant, then so am I. It's no big deal.*

We were no longer throwing rocks at old wine bottles floating down the river in Hot Springs, trying to be the first to break one anymore, but I could get my arms around a little brotherly competition. From that day on I never turned back.

In some ways, neither did Sherman.

IN THE THIRTY-SEVEN YEARS from that day in Hawaii, I have been to every major country on earth and experienced leadership from every angle and approach. I have seen leaders with no fancy titles to generals, senators, cabinet members, even presidents who could have used some time at the knee of my grandmother. I have learned more about human nature in all its beautiful and twisted forms than I could have reasonably expected had I not followed Sherman into the Marine Corps.

I also learned that real leadership is a lost art.

This concept I'm referring to is that old-fashioned, fundamental, old-school leadership where those in charge walk the walk, talk the talk, and still have the confidence and integrity to lead from the heart.

Plenty of people in high places give orders and issue edicts designed to make their subordinates jump. I've seen it every day in the Marine Corps. And in business, politics, even academia, managers, officers, and professors still use the time-worn tool of fear to manipulate people into action or to prevent them from acting at all.

Everyone, from parents and coaches to religious "leaders" and military elites, frequently demand behavior that belies their own actions.

But real leaders, whether in the military, in a corporate or civic setting or taking care of a family, *inspire* people to perform. We are effective leaders when people we lead go that extra mile because it is the right thing to do, and they recognize as much.

There is an old saw that goes, "Ears don't see." Most people are motivated to action far more by what they see than what they hear. That's why genuine leadership is hard to fake. As with anything else, a person can stand out in one of two ways: You can be a character. Or you can demonstrate character.

I am fortunate enough to have become familiar with the latter, first as a child growing up with two exceptionally strong women, then later as a staff noncommissioned officer to men such as Congressional Medal of Honor recipient Lt. Colonel Wesley Fox, Major Butch Morgan, and General James L. Jones, thirty-second Commandant of the United States Marine Corps and later supreme allied commander, Europe, and commander, United States European Command.

I grew up in a time and place that demanded old-fashioned leadership just to survive. Since then I have spent nearly four decades in an environment built on those qualities—honor, commitment, and integrity. A combination of unique life experiences has allowed my career to be like none before me.

Less than one percent of all enlisted Marines attain the status of sergeant major. Sergeants major work for and support the highest-ranking commanders in the Marine Corps, as part of the command structure.

As an enlisted Marine is promoted in rank, his pay grade moves up as well. For example, a private is a Marine pay grade classified as an E-1, or the lowest pay grade. The E designates the Marine as enlisted. The number 1, refers to the pay grade and is an administrative classification used primarily to standardize compensation across the military services.

At the E-8 level, the Marine Corps has two positions that represent different career paths. This means when an E-7 or gunnery sergeant is promoted to an E-8, he can go one of two ways.

If he becomes a master sergeant, then that Marine will work in the same job he has been trained to do until he retires. For example, if he is trained in aviation mechanics, that's where he will work for the rest of his career.

If on the other hand he is selected to go the sergeant major route, then he will become a first sergeant. The path for a first sergeant leads up into the command structure of the Corps. It is the only route a

Marine can take to become the Sergeant Major of the Marines Corps—the very top job for a noncommissioned officer. Only sixteen sergeants major have held that position in the history of the Marines.

By the time I became the fourteenth Sergeant Major of the Marine Corps in 1999, I had been through some of the most challenging leadership training in the military.

I had been on the drill field in San Diego as a senior drill instructor, completed Marine Security Guard School (Embassy School) at Quantico, been detachment (DET) commander at the United States embassy in Copenhagen, Denmark, then afterward returned to become one of the African-American instructors at Embassy School, and worked at the University of Minnesota mentoring future officers. My last stop before heading to El Toro, California, as deputy of the Staff Noncommissioned Officer Academy, was in Puerto Rico as a first sergeant working for Major Butch Morgan.

In very short order—June 1989—I went from deputy to sergeant major of the Staff NCO Academy. I was "frocked," which meant I was made a sergeant major in name, stripe, and responsibility, but I wouldn't be officially paid accordingly until that December.

I moved on to become Sergeant Major of Officer Candidates School (OCS) from May 1991 to June 1994 where I worked first for Colonel Fox and later for then Col. Pete Osmon. Both men embodied the core values of the Marines Corps.

Colonel Fox did two tours of duty in each of two wars, the Korean and Vietnam. He was wounded in Korea and again in Vietnam, the last time in one of the bloodiest battles of the Vietnam War. More than 75 percent of Alpha Company died in a fierce battle that defined Colonel Fox's career and resulted in a Congressional Medal of Honor awarded by President Richard Nixon.

Colonel Fox knew war, and he refused to bend the rules to accommodate anyone as commanding officer of OCS. He was known to be hard core and rigid; nonetheless I watched him walk down a mud trail into the woods near the Potomac River at the edge of the Marine base at Quantico, Virginia, when a young candidate had broken under the stress of one of the most demanding programs in the Marine Corps. Colonel Fox didn't send me, or any other Marine. He went into the woods himself to look for that young candidate.

Colonel Osmon, who went on to become a lieutenant general, brought his own brand of compassion to OCS. We had a terrible incident where one of the instructors, a seasoned and accomplished Marine, molested his stepdaughter. Instead of allowing his wife and her child to suffer through the additional pain and agony of being left alone and financially ruined, Colonel Osmon fought to ensure they were taken care of by the Marine Corps.

As sergeant major of the 31st Marine Expeditionary Unit (MEU) (Special Operations Capable) and later as sergeant major of the 1st Marine Airborne Wing (MAW), both in Okinawa, Japan, from June 1994 to November 1996, I supported the command of one of the "seven jewels" of the Marine Corps.

The seven MEUs are positioned around the world ready to act at a moment's notice. An MEU has every component of the Marine Corps— ground, air, sea, and combat services. It's no secret where an MEU is located at any given moment, but what it is doing there is classified.

IN NOVEMBER 1995, I became sergeant major of the 1st Marine Aircraft Wing, which oversees all airborne activities in the Pacific from Hawaii to Japan.

After serving in that position for a year, I returned to Washington, D.C.

If less than one percent of all Marines become sergeants major, then only a fraction of one percent ever work for a general. I have worked for two. In November 1996, I became sergeant major to the first three-star female lieutenant general in Marine Corps history,

Lt. General Carol Mutter. Lt. General Mutter was in charge of Manpower and Reserve Affairs, the Marine Corps equivalent of human resources.

I assumed manpower would be my final stop and I wanted to leave my mark there, a legacy that would help all those Marines who came after me.

Working for Lt. General Mutter at Marine headquarters certainly had raised my profile, but I have never allowed any job to define my career, one way or another, not even the top job in the Marine Corps.

All Marines aspire to become the top sergeant major of the Marine Corps. I knew I had the qualifications to be considered for the position, but I was focused on trying to learn the eighty-plus programs at Manpower.

I remember Lt. General Mutter being asked about diversity and when was the Marine Corps going to have an African-American in the role of sergeant major.

"I don't know," Lt. General Mutter said. "But I know who would do a good job. The right person for the job is right here."

On July 1, 1999, Lt. General Mutter's comment seemed prescient. I left Manpower to become the fourteenth Sergeant Major of the Marine Corps under General Jones and the first African-American ever to hold that title.

A lot has been made of that last point, though not by me. Intellectually, I understand the historical nature of the fact. Only fifty-three years earlier, in 1946, the Marine Corps commandant at the time affirmed the institution's post-war policy of racial separation. That was five years after President Franklin D. Roosevelt signed Executive Order 8802 and established the Fair Employment Practices Commission, which outlawed racial discrimination by any government agency, including the Marine Corps. And it wasn't until 1983, when General Frank E. Petersen was promoted, that an African-American rose to the rank of three-star general.

Practically, however, I have never been sure why the color of my skin mattered. After all, as a leader I was there to focus on all Marines: white, black, Latino, every color of the rainbow. People from every kind of place and circumstance you can imagine. And some you can't.

I was the highest-ranking noncommissioned officer in the Marine Corps, and the one person in charge day-to-day, reporting directly to the commandant, General Jones. I was there to look out for every Marine, all 212,000 of them. Together with General Jones, we led the Marine Corps with a single purpose: to take care of the men and women whose lives had been entrusted to us.

When General Jones became the supreme allied commander at NATO in 2003, he asked me to join him in Brussels as senior non-commissioned officer for Allied Command Operations, a position that didn't exist until General Jones created it. I became the first sergeant major of the Supreme Allied Command in June 2003 and held the position through July 17, 2006, traveling throughout the world, including multiple trips to the wars in Iraq and Afghanistan.

Initially, I was charged with creating a sergeants major/NCO program throughout the NATO command since none had existed prior. In some ways, the diversity I lent, and the diversity of the experiences that landed me in my role, made it possible for me to navigate multiple cultures and their mores more easily. Within six months, the entire program was introduced and in place, and a transformation had taken place within twenty-six countries.

Noncommissioned officers, who filled the newly created sergeant major positions, were no longer underutilized or deemed inferior to the officer ranks, even among countries with long and storied military histories.

SINCE LEAVING THE MILITARY in July 2006, I have dedicated myself to designing and implementing leadership programs with a personal emphasis both on children in New York and on the military, focused particularly on those at risk.

I am president and chief executive of The 4 DREW (Developing Responsible Educated Winners) Foundation, an organization I've recently started. It is dedicated to supporting children by providing a lifeline to education and life skills through leadership, mentoring, counseling, coaching, and training.

In addition to consulting and speaking engagements for national and multinational corporations and professional organizations, I've served on the 2007 Independent Commission on the Security Forces of Iraq chaired by General Jones.

We presented an honest and blunt assessment of the Iraqi Security Forces' capabilities to Congress in September of 2007. In short, the report stated that the forces, which included the army and police, could not "meaningfully contribute to denying terrorists safe haven," or take over internal security from United States forces within twelve to eighteen months.

I continue to serve on a variety of government and military commissions, including those devoted to the study and prevention of sexual assault and domestic violence, suicide prevention in the military, veteran's affairs, and the Young Marines program.

IN THE END, MY early leadership skills were formed inside that one-story house on Helm Street, at a dinner table surrounded by mismatched chairs, nine brothers and sisters, and my grandmother at the head.

We were taught everything from the Twenty-third Psalm to the Golden Rule at that table, but we understood what it all meant by seeing our mother and grandmother in action every day. They never hesitated to walk the walk.

2

Practice Dinner Table Values:
Respect, Integrity, Discipline

I GREW UP IN A house dominated by black women and then went on to lead one of the most testosterone-fueled and historically white-male-dominated institutions on earth. To anyone who knew Miss Rosa and Miss Ida, that would seem perfectly reasonable.

Miss Rosa was my mother, a woman of considerable beauty and an unmistakable spirit. She had beautiful, dark ebony skin and penetrating eyes. Despite nine pregnancies and ten children—all but two, twins she bore at age forty-six, were born at home with a midwife— she was never bigger than a size six. She took pride in keeping herself up, and although she grew up in the Deep South in the 1930s and 1940s, I don't believe she considered herself less than anyone—white, black, male, or female—for even a minute of her life.

She was a meticulous woman and put herself together in a style and manner of her own design. She loved hats and knew how to cock one just right for maximum effect. When my mother walked, her dress did swing. The term "poetry in motion" should have been reserved for her. For all anyone knew, she was worth $1 million, and Miss Rosa wasn't about to volunteer any information to the contrary.

There's no doubt she had a sharp sense of style, but there's also no question she had a tongue to match. It didn't matter who you were. If you crossed the line between respect and disrespect, Miss Rosa would let you know.

She worked for a group of doctors. If she had to call her boss "Dr. Jackson," then he had to call her "Miss Rosa." It was that simple. My mother cleaned the clinic in the morning, then headed over to the doctors' homes to do domestic work in the afternoon. At night she worked parties at their houses. But she never allowed them any space when it came to what she considered to be respectable behavior.

If one of those doctors said something out of line, even if it was about one of us kids, or if they asked a question Miss Rosa felt was none of their business, she would shut them down like they had just robbed Wells Fargo.

While my grandmother, Ida, never fussed or yelled at any of us, with my mother it was *whack, bam, boom,* and then "get it done." She was nothing if not consistent. My mother never saw a butt she didn't think could use a good spanking. And she could wear your butt out. You didn't want to get on her bad side because then she'd be on your backside. The Marines? No big deal. All they did was yell. My mom would yell at us while she was handing out a beating.

"Why are you crying?" she'd say. "I'll give you something to cry about."

Then, if you didn't cry and took your punishment like a man, she'd still tell you she was going to give you something to cry about.

That woman had total control. And she had to. When you have all those kids with young boys mixed in and not even the shadow of a father, it is a very short walk to chaos. And no way are you going down that road.

As far as I knew, there were never any keys to our house. The screen door always had to be in good shape to keep out the bugs and mosquitoes in the summer. We didn't have any fancy latches or locks, just a hook. It never occurred to anyone to ever lock the door, because then somebody might not be able to get in.

When you walked in the front door, you were in the living room. I remember my mother being proud that the room was "fifteen by fifteen," though we had no idea of the significance of that fact. Off to the side was a large Victrola radio, the kind with a hand-crank phonograph that was about half the size of a modern refrigerator. The mail went on top of the radio.

Growing up as a family, we gathered to watch television, every one of us jockeying to find a chair. My mother and grandmother controlled what we watched and when we watched it. But everybody made sure they were home on Saturday nights to see *Have Gun Will Travel* and *Gunsmoke.* You had to have that dose of Richard Boone and James Arness or you didn't have a good end to your week.

Off to the left, a chair sat next to a small table where the phone was. That was the command center. Nobody sat in that chair except my mother. That's where she did all the family business—and just about everybody else's business as well.

People used to call her the *"New Era"* and the *"Sentinel Record."* Those were the names of the afternoon and morning newspapers in Hot Springs. If there was news to be had, my mother knew about it long before those papers hit the porch.

But she also had these small, soft hands. You would walk by and she'd pull you in with those hands and say, "Give me a kiss." There was no way in the world, no matter what came before or after that moment, that you could leave those arms without knowing to the bottom of your soul that she loved you unconditionally.

Strange as it may sound, there was very little talk about the fact we didn't have a father around the house. It's reasonable to expect some measure of chaos or confusion in a house full of kids and no grown man to help look after them. Not in our house. We were pushed toward reality on that subject, and on anything else we couldn't control.

"It is the way it is," we were told. "No one can change the facts. Move on."

And that's exactly what we did.

When you think of a mother who had ten kids and never married, one might imagine a person inclined to take the easy way out. But that wasn't Miss Rosa. My mother never allowed herself to be a victim of anything, including her own actions. We were her children, and she worked three jobs seven days a week to make sure our needs were met. She brought us into this world, and she never abandoned that responsibility by latching onto worldly excuses.

Now some people might look at the facts of her life negatively. Ten kids, no father? I saw something different. I saw strength and character in the way she lived her life. You can call us mistakes or the result of her poor decisions, but my mother never expected a handout. She never wavered, no matter how hard times got and no matter how long they stayed that way.

We never had to live in a dark house because the lights had been shut off, and we never went to sleep cold in the winter because the heat couldn't be turned on. None of us could ever say we went to bed without enough food to eat. As a matter of fact, no one in the neighborhood could say they were hungry as long as Miss Rosa was around.

She would get up early in the morning and cook her famous buttermilk pound cake, or make a couple of pies. Then she would let them sit there out on the dining room table for anyone who happened to come by. Neighbor kids came to the door all the time.

"What smells so good?"

"Go get yourself a plate," she'd say. "And go sit at the dining room table and have yourself some."

IF MY MOTHER HAD Cicely Tyson features, then my grandmother Ida's were more like those of Oprah Winfrey. Ida was the granddaughter of a freed slave who essentially raised herself. Her mother, my great-grandmother, died when Ida was a little girl. Her father and his brothers owned a large tract of land on one side of what became the Interstate, just opposite land owned by the Rockefellers in North Little Rock. He worked that land, and he expected his daughter to do the same no matter her age.

She came to work naturally in a way few men do. She'd hitch up a mule and plow a field or pick cotton all day long. I never knew a man who could outwork my grandmother. It didn't matter whether it was weeding a garden, using a hatchet, or driving a nail. There wasn't a man around who could do it any better than Ida could. I never saw my grandmother get old because she was always stronger than us. She was rarely ever sick and always had the appetite of a working man.

I remember the time my brother-in-law James was home on leave from the Navy and staying with my grandmother. She had moved back to Little Rock by this time to take over her father's property following his passing. One night, she asked James if he would help her move a large boulder in her front yard.

James later told us he was lying in bed early the next morning when he heard strange sounds coming from outside. By the time he jumped up, dressed, and made it out, she had moved that boulder all the way across the yard by herself. That was Ida. She might ask you for help once, but she never depended on anybody to do anything she couldn't do for herself.

My grandmother didn't need anything to make herself feel special. She'd work all day, then come home, throw on a big old shirt, an old pair of coveralls, a straw hat, put a twig in her mouth, and go to work in the vegetable garden out back or in one of her flower gardens. My mother was an inside worker, but my grandmother could go both ways from sun up to sun down and never change expressions. She had the kind of strong hands that come from hard work. So, too, did my older sisters, Ida and Ruby.

Though I never saw my grandmother wear an ounce of nail polish, you could see life in those hands, and everything she touched could feel it, too. My grandmother never bought a flower in her life, but she had flowers blooming all over the house, inside and out. She could take a pinch of a plant or the stem of a dying rose and nurse it back to its full splendor.

Because of how Ida approached her work, I never knew being a maid or a domestic was considered a low-level job. Ida worked so hard, with such attention to detail, that everyone respected her. She might have been nothing more than the fourth-floor janitor at Hot Springs High School, but my grandmother carried herself with dignity among all those white teachers, many of whom had educated Bill Clinton. I guarantee you, those who are still living would remember her as well as they remember the former president.

On Saturdays, she would finish cleaning at school, then head to Miss Mackey's house to do domestic work. Miss Johnny May Mackey was the principal at Hot Springs High. You might think of my grandmother as her servant, but when Miss Mackey passed away, Ida was there at her bedside holding her hand. She was the only person Miss Mackey allowed in the room.

My grandmother had a way of making people feel good about themselves, though she never thought less of herself in the process. Society might have labeled her a maid, but she was far more than that to everyone she touched. She never gave two seconds thought about being a black janitor in an all-white school or a domestic, cleaning houses in a neighborhood we couldn't live in. From her perspective, hers was an honest livelihood that allowed her to provide for her family.

Those women, my mother and grandmother, prepared me well for the Marine Corps—and everything that came with it. I'd see guys yelling and screaming and I knew they weren't even close to being as tough as my mother or as strong as my grandmother.

Ida was responsible, she was dependable, and she was capable. She never wavered on those principles. Every Saturday, she would get her hair done at Mrs. Wilson's salon because she "had to be presentable" at school. The salon, inside the back of Mrs. Wilson's house, also sold candy, as did a number of houses in our neighborhood.

When Ida walked out of our house Monday morning and headed down the road to work, everyone saw a lady. When she pulled off her coat and put on her work clothes, they saw a dependable and relentless worker. When she walked out of there and headed home that night, she was back to Miss Ida. They depended on her for a maid, but they respected her as Miss Ida.

As the leader of our family, my grandmother sat at the head of the dinner table in the dining room. My mother never sat at the table. Her domain was the kitchen. After cooking, Miss Rosa would retreat into the living room and eat sitting quietly in her chair. That's when my grandmother would take charge. My brother, being older than me, got to sit at the other end of the table as if he were the man of the house. Everyone else had an assigned seat, too, and the seating generally went by seniority.

The dinner table is where my grandmother laid out her expectations for us as well as those of the larger society. She taught us about the Bible at that table and recited the Lord's Prayer. She told us all about the Last Supper and explained the rituals around Easter and Christmas.

But mostly Ida massaged positive messages into our hearts and minds. That's how my grandmother worked, from the head to the heart. These were simple truths delivered with the wisdom of a woman who had found peace and comfort in her life by completely accepting exactly who she was.

For all of us, it was soul food delivered one morsel at a time. These are some of her life lessons:

"Have patience and compassion in your heart for those who are struggling. Nobody wakes up in the morning thinking about how they can make your day miserable."

"Never compromise your integrity by cheating another person."

"Courtesy can take you a long way. Always be courteous."

"Never value anyone based on color, size, age, or weight."

"Your word is your bond."

"Integrity is the strength to tell the truth."

SHE TAUGHT US BY example. We saw her put those words into action every day without the slightest hedge or modification.

If a couple of us got into a scuffle, my mother would say, "Just don't let me see any blood."

But to my grandmother, fighting between siblings was unacceptable. Families didn't fight one another. She preached kindness and love.

"If no one else in the world loves you, at least you know you have sisters and brothers who do," she'd say. "If one of you has anything at all, then find a way to share it with everyone else."

To this day, my siblings have never forgotten those words.

Rather than allowing us to focus on what we didn't have, or where we couldn't go, she brought us together by talking about what we did have. That was her way of neutralizing any concerns we might have had about the racial realities of the time, or the reality of our day-to-day struggle to survive.

Working in the garden with my grandmother or taking care of the animals out back wasn't just about food—it was about nurturing life. I learned how to work the soil in such a way that it provided the best opportunity for the seeds to rise up from the ground. She would sit us down and pull out the *Farmer's Almanac* to see when the right time to plant was. Then she'd show us how to soak seeds in an old bucket of water so that the seeds didn't have to sit in the soil for three weeks before they started to grow.

We had to walk around the garden to get to the animals. It was important to be responsible with the animals because if we left a gate open, we knew they would head straight for the vegetables. So we used chicken wire or an old mattress to block the opening to keep the goats inside. We took a couple of tree branches and made posts. I remember making a gate that led into what we called the chicken yard. I used a piece of leather as a hinge until we were able to find an old door being thrown away. We took that lumber home, removed the hinges, then used the wood for something else.

The rabbits were kept in fifty old crates. We had a couple of cast-iron buckets that my siblings and I filled with water from the house. Then we'd carry them two at a time back out across the yard, maybe fifty to a hundred yards, pouring the water into old coffee cans inside the rabbit coops.

We fed and watered the animals, milked the cow and the goats. All these things had to be done every day, and my grandmother would remind us we should be proud of the fact we had done a day's work.

We created our fun out of whatever we could find. You eyed a new mop or broom coming into the house because you knew sooner or later that was going to be the horse you rode when you played cowboys and Indians with your siblings. The broom was a better catch because the pole was a little longer and easier to ride. We'd skip rocks across, or throw old wine bottles into the creek and stand on the banks trying to shatter them with small rocks from the shore.

I never had to get into shape physically when I entered the Marine

Corps because we worked like grown men and women at home long before our time. Being fit was part of our upbringing. My siblings and I would toss bails of hay into the loft of the feedhouse for the calves, haul bags of feed for the chickens, and carry pails of water wherever they were needed.

I remember coming home from the Corps one time and thinking how all that training had to have made me even stronger. Then I reached down, grabbed a bail of hay, and thought, *Wow. How did I do that all those years?*

It was a different kind of strong when you were doing what we were doing every day. But it was all part of our education, all part of those dinner table values.

"No one can take away knowledge," Ida would tell us. "Somebody might take away your car, house, and even money if you make poor choices, but your intellect will always be yours alone. That's how you get to the next level in all facets of your life."

While they fostered positive thinking in all of us, neither my mother nor my grandmother ever devalued what they did for a living. They never told us to get ahead so we didn't have to be a janitor or work cleaning other people's houses. In our home, there was dignity and honor in any job if you held yourself to the highest standards. Being excellent in what you do was the first ingredient in their for-mula to improve our lives.

What made these sermons so powerful was witnessing those women live exactly what they preached. They approached every activ-ity with pride and were rewarded with respect from people far outside our neighborhood. If Miss Ida was supposed to clean your house and you were out of town, no one had to worry about how that work would be done. Her performance didn't change whether you were in that house watching or you were a thousand miles away on vacation.

I remember one of the janitors at the high school complaining to Ida about the mess "those kids" made every day.

My grandmother listened politely before she responded. "If those kids don't make their messes every day," she said, "then we don't have a job cleaning up after them."

I mentioned these "dinner table values" to a group of adults at a seminar I led in Park City, Utah, a while ago. When I finished, a young woman raised her hand and shook her head.

She told me that it wasn't possible for her to think the way I did, since we were raised so differently. I had my mom, my grandmother, my sisters, and brother to learn from. This woman, on the other hand, said she had no one.

"I have raised myself since as long as I can remember," she said. "We didn't even have a dinner table. And even if we did, there wasn't anyone around worth listening to. So where do all those values come from if there isn't even a place for them to be presented?"

But the dinner table I'm talking about is not necessarily the piece of furniture in a kitchen or dining room. It is the center of gravity in your life. It's the place you hold on to when everything else seems to be spinning out of control. It's what allows you to have peace with yourself and others. It extends from your home to your neighborhood to the rest of your community. It's where you find your compass and learn how to use it.

I learned a lot around that old dining room table on Helm Street, but I learned even more watching my grandmother work, and seeing how my mother held our family together against a torrent of challenges, economic and otherwise. I found my dinner table on the football field with a coach named Ross Rosborough, and I found it again in the military with men such as Butch Morgan.

Where was the dinner table for that young woman in Park City? I couldn't answer that question for her. But I know she can find it, I'm certain of that much. She was a lawyer, so she had found her way to some measure of achievement.

The values that inspire good leadership are all around us if we take the time to pay attention. And if you respect the difference between right and wrong, and honor the ideas of personal integrity and character, people who share those values will gravitate toward you.

Most of us know intuitively what the right decision is in any given moment. Acting on our intuition is the difference between leading and being led around. And after the education and training I received at home, I wasn't about to be led around.

I learned how to lead others well by basing my actions on the power and value of those dinner table values from long ago.

3

Impress Yourself First: Set Your Standards High

HE ONLY OLDER MALE around our house for most of my life was only eighteen months older than me, and no one would have confused either of us with a man. That didn't mean we grew up without a clear vision of what it meant to be one. My grandmother had so perfected her approach to life that the absence of a father never translated into an absence of leadership.

Between her influence and that of Coach Ross Rosborough, I had the equivalent of a Harvard education in manhood. Ross was an assistant football coach and mentor to young boys, particularly those without a father at home. He had three of his own children, took care of his mother, and became one of the most popular and well-known people in the entire community for all the right reasons.

Neither Ida nor Ross would ever change their approach to impress anyone. Both started with the Golden Rule—treat others how you want to be treated—and never wavered. Somewhere along the way, I figured out that if I didn't live my life according to my own values, then I could never be true to anyone else.

In retrospect, I learned a lot about setting my own standards high from these two adults. If I was willing to surrender my dreams because the road seemed too long or the demands too great, then the dream business had no room for me. Circumstances constantly reminded me not to expect anything if I wasn't willing to work for it. The examples of Ida and Ross helped me understand how to work for what I wanted and enjoy life at the same time.

Physically, my grandmother and Ross couldn't have been more different. My grandmother never needed fancy clothes or name brand anything to make her feel special. Her beauty radiated from the inside out, and it caught the eye of everyone she meant. She might have a spot of snuff in her lip or a toothpick hanging out of her mouth as she worked outside, but nothing altered the glow that came from her.

Ross was a different story. At a time when African-Americans were just being introduced to Afros, Ross wore his dark, wavy hair long and combed it straight back like Elvis. He was a handsome man with light-brown skin and an outgoing personality. Ross worked as a bellman at the Avanelle Motor Lodge downtown on Central Avenue. He knew everyone in Hot Springs, adults and children, and it didn't matter who you were or the color of your skin, you knew Ross.

In one way, Ross and my grandmother were the same. They could take you into the palm of their hand and educate you about life without ever squeezing too hard. They used just the right amount of pressure to get your attention without ever making it sound like a lecture. They put more time and love into me than I ever could have paid back to them.

Ross had a way of motivating us to see alternatives, ways to improve our lives. He'd talk to us about all aspects of life, but especially about our mothers.

"Always love your mom," he'd say. "Never ever make your mom second in your life. Never hurt your mother by doing stupid things. Never let her read about you in the newspaper because of something you did wrong."

His words inspired me to live up to a high moral code.

He didn't just speak those words. You could see he lived them in the way he treated his own mother. She was his priority. He would drop anything to take care of whatever his mother needed.

Coach Ross mentored me in practical matters, too. He helped me buy my first car when I was sixteen years old. I went on to use some of these same lessons to mentor young Marines later on in my own career.

A few weeks before my junior year started in 1968, Ross took me over to a used car lot where I picked out a 1964 gold Chevy Impala with four doors and a front bench, no bucket seats. To this day, I'm not sure how I was able to secure the $800 loan from the owner of the car lot. I know Ross told the man I would pay back the loan, and I'm pretty sure Ross backed that up by telling the guy he'd pay if I failed.

My car note was forty-six dollars a month. I was already working two jobs: one as a busboy at the Avanelle after school, the other cleaning yards on the weekend. But once I bought my Chevy Impala, I added a third gig: I started my own taxi service before and after school. And I made sure I saved the first forty-six dollars I made each month to repay my loan. I didn't even consider going to a movie or getting a hamburger until I had every penny to satisfy my loan.

RIGHT AROUND THIS TIME, integration came to Hot Springs, but you needed a car to find it. The newly integrated high school we were to attend was located more than five miles outside of town. In my house and others on the block, the idea of going to school with white kids was trumped by logistics. Specifically, how were you actually going to get to school?

I knew none of the kids in my neighborhood had a car. That left two options. They could borrow their mother's, assuming she had one, or they could catch the bus. There was no chance of any of them borrowing their father's truck. The bus cost twenty-five cents each way, but you had to walk to the bus stop.

I thought that if I provided door-to-door service for fifty cents each way, I could find regular customers. Even though I charged a little more than the bus—a hundred percent more now that I think about it—my proposition was straightforward: I would pick you up at home and drop you off at school on time every day. I just had to find the right customers who would appreciate the benefits of my service. Boys, however, were out. I knew that the first time one of them got into my car.

"Hey man, how fast can you go in this car? Come on, step on it."

I knew then their interests were not aligned with what was best for me. I didn't want their negative thoughts around me, and I couldn't afford to be perceived in a bad light, particularly by adults or the company who held my loan. I was establishing my own brand, and it would hurt my business—and my integrity.

My approach wasn't technically sophisticated, but I knew boys were not the right clientele. I knew I wouldn't find any joy in getting drunk. I knew what a drunk person looked like and I knew how one acted. My grandfather, Smokey, loved to drink, and when I was young he made every one of us miserable when he did. I knew I would find no joy in trying to be a cool guy by smoking cigarettes, either.

It wasn't like I had sleepless nights coming to those conclusions. There wasn't enough peer pressure in the world to make me choose those things over the positive examples I had been exposed to. I got up every morning with a very clear understanding of what I wanted to do and how I wanted to run my life. My standards were high because that's how I wanted them—I was out to impress myself first.

Because of that I knew instinctively to stick to girls. I knew girls. I grew up with a house full of them. I knew they wanted every extra minute they could find in the morning to put on their makeup, to get their lipstick just right. Every minute they saved by not walking to the bus stop, particularly if the weather was poor, was a bonus. They liked the idea. More important, their parents did, too.

All those pennies I had invested by trying to be a good kid were adding up. The parents trusted me to take care of their daughters. The additional cost was no problem. I had five customers, all girls, for the entire school year.

By the end of the first week of school, I was more than halfway to the forty-six dollars I needed for my loan payment that month. I quickly added another shift taking my oldest sister, Ida Mae, to work. When her coworker Miss Maggie wanted a ride, I added another. Every one of my riders paid, no questions asked, because I was reliable. (Of course my mother and grandmother rode for free at all times.)

If I was going to pick up Miss Maggie for work at 7:00 A.M., then I was in front of Miss Maggie's house at 7:00 A.M. Now Miss Maggie wasn't always on time, so I had to explain to her the ramifications of her tardiness on my schedule. I was a kid telling a grown woman to be on time. I told her straight up in a very calm, confident voice. This was a business.

After school, I dropped the girls off at their homes and went to work at the Avanelle. They all knew I didn't have time for any of them to hang around their lockers, or spend time talking with their boyfriends. They had to be inside the car in their seats when I got there. If they weren't, then they would be catching the bus home with no refund.

I established the ground rules, and the girls followed them. That's the difference. I knew the boys wouldn't follow any rules. They would have tried to test the boundaries every day. And I didn't have time for that. Now when the girls wanted to stick around and hang out with their boyfriends, they didn't like the rules. But I knew their parents did.

⇒ ⇒ ⇒

MR. HUNTER AND HIS wife Dorothy lived around the corner. They had five girls, and I drove a couple of them to school. I knew Mr. Hunter went down to a filling station on Saturdays to work on cars. The black police officers, some of the teachers and deacons from our church, hung out there on Saturdays, too. So I'd drive up, park my car in front of the pumps, and say hello. "Don't worry about that gas," Mr. Hunter would say. "You fill it up. I'll take care of it."

Now I had no overhead! My tank was full and my reputation just got a boost in front of all those men, most of whom were the police.

I had fat pockets in those days. I started out saving twenty-five cents of every dollar I made. Eventually, I was saving seventy-five cents of every dollar. I paid off my car by Christmas, less than five months after I brought my car home.

Just inside the front door of our house was a bookshelf I made in shop class. It was a beautiful walnut bookshelf about four feet tall with four shelves, a curved top, and plywood back. I made sure it was well sanded, stained, and polished before I brought it home. If I was going to make something in woodshop, then I wanted to make something impressive—something that impressed me. We didn't need another shoe-shine kit, which is what everyone else made. The bookshelf ended up in our house as a piece of furniture. All the bills were placed in a little bowl that sat next to a vase on the top shelf. My mother opened all the bills, then put them on the other side in another little bowl.

I can't explain the feeling I had the first time I took one of those bills out of the pile. Now it was my turn to give back.

"You seen the water bill?"

"Yes, mam, I paid it already."

That's when I felt like a man.

When the Vietnam War officially ended with the signing of the Paris Peace Accords on January 27, 1973, President Richard Nixon gave military personnel a substantial pay raise. For those at my level the raise amounted to a 100 percent increase. I started sending $150 a month back home to my mother. I never stopped, not even after I got married and needed every cent I could find. The last check went to my mom twenty-five years later—up until she passed away in January 1998. I know there were times when that small amount of money made a big difference in my mother's life.

MY MOTHER WAS ALWAYS conscious of how we conducted ourselves outside our home, particularly how we dressed. We didn't have much at all growing up, but that didn't mean we couldn't have our shoes shined and our clothes cleaned.

The summer when Sherman and I were around twelve and thirteen years old, my mother sent us to my great-grandfather's farm in North Little Rock. She made sure her sons were dressed in suits and ties with freshly shined shoes for the trip. We took the Trailways bus from Hot Springs to Little Rock, got off at the bus station, then took a taxi to North Little Rock where my great-grandfather Pete lived. Then we headed to the fields. It didn't matter to my mother that we were going to a farm to work all summer. We had to be presentable.

The same rules applied for church and school. We had to shine our shoes, not just the ones we wore to church, but our school shoes, too. My mother taught us how to present ourselves to the world in keeping with her values. We didn't have much, but there was no room for excuses. Take pride in the way you present yourself. The message was no more complicated than that.

That's why the old expression about having one chance to make a first impression is so true. It's important to be conscious of how you present yourself whether at work or out in the larger community. There is nothing wrong with personal expression, but perception matters. I remind high school students to ask themselves these questions:

Do I present myself in a way that encourages others to be around me?

Does the fact I wear sweat pants with an old T-shirt and an iPod hanging out my ear keep others away?

The way you present yourself shouldn't change around your family, your coworkers, or anyone else with whom you come into contact. In other words, if you turn into a bum or do things you wouldn't otherwise do in front of your children or in front of your spouse when no one is looking, then you don't have enough self-discipline or pride.

It comes down to understanding the consequences of each decision we make. The results of all the decisions accumulate one way or another. It's your responsibility to make them add up positively.

Impress yourself first.

How do you value yourself? Is your self-worth defined by the opinions of others? It is determined by how well you compare to the guy in the next cubicle?

When I played football in the Marine Corps, I wanted to be John Mackey. John was a six foot five, two-hundred-fifty-pound, Hall of Fame tight end for the Baltimore Colts (before they moved to Indianapolis). He had incredible speed and agility for a man of his size. I watched players like Mackey, Jim Taylor, and Jim Brown—big powerful men. They ran over people and knocked the snot out of them in the process. They were especially brutal in a game defined by brutality. I thought, *Okay, that's football. You run over people. That's what I'm going to do.*

That's how I saw myself. The only problem with that picture was that I stood five feet ten inches and weighed one hundred fifty pounds. I was too light in the pants to run over anyone. Once I recognized and accepted my strengths—speed, agility, and quickness—suddenly I had a chance to play. I went from the bench to becoming a starting tailback because I acknowledged my abilities, accepted my limitations, and embraced the possibilities.

That's a difficult concept for many people to grasp, particularly in a culture that tells us that success is driving a BMW or Mercedes, while driving a Neo or Geo represents failure. There's nothing wrong with being a Neo or Geo as long as you are the best one on the road. (And with the price of hydrocarbons today, a Neo or Geo is a lot cheaper to operate than a $100,000, eight-cylinder luxury car.) All we really need a car for is to get from one place to another safely and efficiently.

Life isn't much different. The journey should be safe and joyful. If you aren't smart enough or strong enough to be president of the United States, then set your goals to be the best governor or mayor you can be. If you aren't the principal of the school, then be the best teacher. It's all about the journey—and that journey will be the most successful if you accept who you are. If you are trying to be John Mackey, rather than relying on your gifts, say, of quickness and speed, then you are putting yourself in a position to be unhappy.

It's no different than deciding you want to be a doctor, but instead of going to college and studying biology and chemistry, you head straight to the hospital hoping to perform surgery.

Accepting who you are and performing to the best of your capabilities eliminates obstacles. Excuses become irrelevant. My mother never allowed even the smallest space for an excuse. That option doesn't exist in the military, either. If you think about it, excuses don't fly in the rest of life, either. Sooner or later, effort, discipline, and performance conspire to produce results, good or bad.

The store down the street only pays minimum wage? So that's why you're going to sell drugs and put yourself in jail? When I was young, I preferred to work for minimum wage and go to bed at night knowing the police weren't going to kick down my door and tear the house up looking for a cigar box full of drug money. To me that was freedom.

I wasn't trying to suck up to adults any more than I tried to befriend my superiors in the Marine Corps. I wanted to be judged by my actions and the results those actions produced. I wanted the freedom that came with respect.

When I was growing up, I was free to go and do whatever I wanted because my mother knew I wasn't going to abuse that privilege. Adults trusted me because I was willing to meet their expectations. It sounds corny, but to me it just made my life so much easier. I couldn't bare an adult not wanting to be around me because I was a bad apple. I couldn't deal with that. If I came over to your house and sat on the porch, then I came to listen. I wanted to learn. I wanted to hear what older people had to say because they had been around. They had experienced aspects of life that were still way down the road for me.

I used to go down to Mrs. Hunter's house and sit out on the front porch with her on a couple of old metal chairs. I wasn't there to see her girls like a lot of other boys my age. I had grown up with them. They were like sisters to me. Mrs. Hunter was like another mom. I came to talk to her about my dreams, what I wanted in life, or how I was going to go about realizing those dreams. I soaked up practical knowledge and advice from whomever I respected. That's how I learned to set my standards.

Mrs. Hunter would talk to me about what it meant to be a man by planting tiny seeds in my mind.

"I'm going to make sure I have my own house. Then I'm going to buy all my own furniture. I'm going to have everything in place before I get married," I remember saying once.

She listened as I talked.

"You know," she said, "you might not want to do it that way. Maybe you want to save your money and wait until you are married so you and your wife can pick out all those things together."

That was an invaluable slice of wisdom since I didn't grow up with two parents making joint decisions. I watched my mother do it all on her own. If we needed something, my mother made a decision, then acted on it.

"A man takes care of his family," Mrs. Hunter would tell me. "A man does what is right because it is right, whether anyone knows it or not. A man honors his wife and provides leadership to his family. A man is someone the rest of the family can count on to do what needs to be done. He's a respectable person not just to his family, but to those in the community, at church. Those are the kinds of things you might want to consider when you think about becoming a man."

EVEN THOUGH I ADVANCED very quickly in the military, I never forgot what I learned from Mrs. Hunter. Still, I had no desire to get married in those early career days. As a young Marine, I knew I couldn't give someone's daughter anything more than her father was already providing. I didn't want to give anyone the title of wife if I couldn't carry the title of husband.

It wasn't until I became a senior drill instructor in San Diego that the thought of marriage even entered my mind. When it did, I had almost nothing to do with it. Rita and I met in the fall of 1974 thanks to a chance meeting.

In many ways, I was becoming all those things Mrs. Hunter talked to me about. I was in the best physical condition of my life in one of the glamour positions in the military, senior drill instructor. I was so focused on turning out great recruits that I didn't immediately recognize the significance of a major promotion.

A buddy of mine, Staff Sergeant Edwards, came up to me one day with news the two of us were being meritoriously promoted. I was being promoted from sergeant to staff sergeant. He was being promoted to gunnery sergeant.

"We are the baddest dudes here," he said. "Of all the people on this base they chose to promote us!"

It took a while for it to sink in. I was so busy thinking about how I could positively affect the recruits in my platoon that I didn't realize the significance of the promotion. This was an accelerated promotion, which meant I was moving up ahead of schedule and faster than my peers. Most of my peers were still corporals who had another three to five years before they made staff sergeant. I was doing it in just over four years. Unbelievable.

But I had no one really with whom to share the good news. I called my mother and she was happy for me, but I knew the significance of the Marine Corps' rank structure meant nothing to her. So I decided to go along with my buddy now Gunnery Sergeant Edwards to the military exchange, which was like our Macy's. It's where military personnel buy just about anything they need from clothes and household items to electronics and bedding.

Edwards was trying to meet a girl who worked there.

"I know this girl at the exchange I'm trying to talk to, but her sister keeps getting in the way," he said. "Why don't you come along so you can run interference for me."

I had nothing better to do, so we headed over to the exchange where Rita's sister, Lucy—the one he was interested in—was sitting out on the patio. I had been given a briefing on Rita. "She doesn't like military guys, so she's got her nose in the air. She's a little stuffy. But you have to try to talk to her."

I went inside the exchange and bought a couple of magazines, or books as I call them. I bought *Jet* magazine, which had Marvin Gaye on the cover of the November 1974 issue. Then I went back outside to sit down.

Rita Winfree came out of the exchange on a break with a little bag in her hand. Her mother had passed away in August. Lucy, her older sister, lived in San Diego and after returning home to Virginia for the funeral, she brought her three younger sisters—Rita, Debbie and Elanda—back with her to California. Celia, Lucy's twin, was married and stayed back in Virginia with her family.

Rita introduced herself, and I said hello. As she sat down, I wondered, *What kind of person is she?*

Then she asked to see my *Jet* magazine.

Now I have this thing about magazines. If I buy one, then I want to be the first one to read it. My daughter, Portia, has the same quirkiness. I have to be the one to break it open for the first time, particularly if I just bought it.

But I had to be a gentleman, so I gave it to Rita. I noticed she was a very pleasant young lady. I could tell she was savvy, smart. We talked for twenty to thirty minutes. I knew she was very protective of her sister Lucy, who happened to be married to a Marine.

"Maybe I'll call you some time," I said as we were leaving.

She gave me her phone number, which she swears to this day was a fake number. I don't want to dispute facts with my wife, but incredibly the "fake" number worked.

In the weeks that followed, Rita claims I bought more appliances and household items than any man needed, all so I could come by the exchange and see her. That's not true. I needed all those things because I was a single man living in an apartment and I didn't want it to look like a barracks.

I finally asked her out to lunch at Burger King. I noticed she ordered a junior Whopper and she barely ate it. Later on, Lucy told me that Rita didn't know whether I was broke or not, so she didn't order her usual regular Whopper. She figured the junior version wouldn't cost me as much and she didn't "want to embarrass" me.

That's the day I knew she was the right kind of person for me. I could see all those qualities that reminded me of my grandmother and my older sisters, Ida and Ruby. She instinctively put the feelings of others ahead of her own. That was enough to get me interested, but then Rita had her own touch of class.

Eventually I listened to the advice of my grandmother, who always said to only marry someone "who will pull the wagon in the same direction as you." I knew I had found that person. It was not like I had been standing around before this with a checklist, but I knew what I didn't want. Then I met Rita, and she had no agenda. She wasn't even considering marriage. As a matter of fact, she wasn't even considering me.

But over the next four years, our relationship grew and we became extremely close, though her younger sister Debbie still wasn't sure anyone was good enough for her Rita. Debbie, who was a senior in high school when Rita and I met, called me McMichael from the time we started dating until at least twelve years into our marriage.

Rita and I were scheduled to go out to a New Year's Day dinner in 1975. By this time, I had been working so hard preparing my platoon for final drill the next day that I couldn't keep my eyes open. I was so tired that I literally kept falling asleep as I drove us to dinner.

"Why don't you just go home," Rita told me. "I'll take your car home with me."

The next day a buddy drove me into work. When final drill was over, I had him take me home so I could call Rita and get my car back.

"Hey, Debbie, where's Rita?" I asked. "Is she at work? Could you just tell her to pick me up at my place when she gets home?"

Then Lucy got on the phone and told me Rita had gone home to Virginia to visit her sister Celia, the only sister to stay behind. Fortunately, I got on a plane and headed to Washington, D.C., for a leadership academy. Soon after I got the whole story from Rita. When I returned to California, Rita remained in Richmond for a while so Celia wouldn't be alone.

I went by the apartment Rita had shared with her family every day to hang out with Debbie, Lucy, and Elanda. Eventually they all moved to Monterey where Lucy's husband was now in the Army. I drove eight hours up the coast every Friday and eight hours back down the coast every Sunday to see Rita, who had come back, and the rest of the family.

Finally, in August 1977, Rita and I were married in a chapel on the Fort Ord military base near Monterey. I was living the dream life. I had a black 1974 Cutless Supreme I had bought for $4,600, an apartment, and Rita back with me in the Southern California sun.

I'VE ALWAYS TAKEN PRIDE in establishing and defining my own standards. Though I've never looked down on anyone who doesn't share them, I've never allowed anyone to alter them either. When I joined the Marine Corps, I refined my principles even further. I never wanted to be one of the many trying to live up to a commander's expectations. I wanted to be the one raising the bar and exceeding expectations.

So I guess the same sense of knowing who the right person is could be said of General Jones when it came time for him to select the fourteenth Sergeant Major of the Marines Corps. General Jones was the incoming Commandant of the Marine Corps in 1999. The Marine Corps forms a board comprised of colonels and generals. The board convenes to look at all the sergeants major in various support positions throughout the Marine Corps in order to choose the next sergeant major.

Among the criteria is the amount of experience candidates have working with high-ranking generals. That analysis thins the ranks significantly. From a group of about 100 to 110, the list is pared down to up to five final candidates.

Everyone knows when the board is in session. The military, like all large organizations, is inherently political. But it's also largely rigid and disciplined when it comes to promotions, particularly at the level of Sergeant Major of the Marine Corps.

Though I was aware of the process, I wasn't focused on the outcome at the time. All kinds of rumors were circulating, and the *Marine Corps Times,* a newspaper that comes out once a week, was speculating as to who might be on the short list. The board usually meets for four or five days and then releases a message with the names of the final candidates.

Now this is a very big deal in the Marine Corps. I was given all kinds of advice if I were to end up being a candidate. I was told how to smile, how to talk about the hallmarks of the Marine Corps—honor, courage, and commitment.

In the end, when I was given the opportunity to interview, I decided to be myself. I knew the foundation upon which I had built my career was created long before I ever joined the Marine Corps. I had strengthened that foundation by incorporating discipline and my own sense of excellence along with lessons from some great leaders. But I never banked the value of my military service up to that point, or the value of the balance of my career, on whether or not I was selected.

Becoming Sergeant Major of the Marine Corps, the highest ranking NCO in the Corps, wasn't life or death. Just to be considered was for me a privilege. I wasn't going to spend hours trying to figure out what General Jones wanted to hear or what kind of fancy buzzwords I needed to use to capture his heart and soul. I was Al McMichael. If he wanted me to be his sergeant major, fine. If he didn't, then I was fine with that decision, too.

The first interview took place inside the Pentagon. When the time came, General Jones, for the most part, allowed me to talk.

If he was looking for a sergeant major who is concerned about weapons, tanks, bombs, and ammunition, then I wasn't the man for him I told him honestly. But if he wanted someone who is concerned about the people we led, their welfare, the quality of life of their spouses and children, and someone who cares about making sure there are educational opportunities, proper pay, and medical support, somebody that will try to say yes more than he says no, that's me.

General Jones really didn't say much to me at all. He wanted to make sure Rita would support the kind of travel that came with the job. I knew she would because she had always been a team player when it came to my career.

A few days later, a second release went out. Five candidates had been reduced to two. The short list became even shorter. Then we waited.

Then a second interview was scheduled at Quantico, where I worked. This time General Jones was in a transmitting mode. He asked direct questions that didn't require much more than a yes or no answer.

When it was over, I went right back to work.

Everyone wanted to know how the interview went, what General Jones had said. I never bought into all that. I had to get on with life. I couldn't just sit on that pony hoping to whip it across the finish line.

I received calls from people all over the world. They were more excited than I was. I enjoyed talking to General Jones and I thought if he enjoyed our discussions as much as I did, then everything would be fine. Beyond that, I had work to do.

One morning, I came into the office after a run. Lt. General Jack Klemp, who had replaced Lt. General Carol Mutter at Manpower, caught me coming through the door.

"Sergeant Major, General Jones called. He wants to talk to you."

"Okay, sir."

I took a shower and got dressed. When I came out of the locker room, General Klemp was waiting.

"Sergeant Major, General Jones has called again."

"Okay, sir."

"Now get into your office and sit there until he calls back."

"Yes, sir."

About thirty minutes later, the call came through that General Jones was on the line.

"Good morning, Sergeant Major. I want to congratulate you on becoming the fourteenth Sergeant Major of the Marine Corps. Do you want to accept the job?"

"Yes, sir, I do."

"Okay, then. I'll give you a few days to get your head around it all, and we'll talk then."

I thanked him, then I called Rita. I had no idea it would mean so much to her. We never really talked about military rank that often. I never came home as the Great Santini, so I had no idea how special my promotion was to her.

WHEN THE COMMANDANT PRESENTS the Sword of Office to the incoming Sergeant Major of the Marine Corps, he repeats the same words spoken to every new sergeant major.

"I hereby give into your charge the Sword of Office of the Sergeant Major of the Marine Corps, symbolizing the proud traditions which distinguish the Sergeant Major of the Corps. Take this sword and wear it honorably. Guard and cherish it as you guard and cherish the things for which it stands. Deliver it untarnished to your successors, and let your successors deliver it to theirs, and let it thus remain the bright emblem of your office."

General Jones and I have never looked back. It's as if we have known one another our whole lives. We might have traveled on different roads, but the values we share are exactly the same. We've done a lot of good things together, and I can honestly say we have been on the same page for the entire book. Together we agreed on what needed to be done, then I went out and took action: implementing, enforcing, and supporting those policies.

MY GREAT-GRANDFATHER USED TO say, "Courtesy will take you a long way." Today I substitute the word "citizenship" when I pass that advice along.

I used to tell young people in the military that negative thoughts and actions produce similar outcomes. You have to learn to purge yourself of toxic thoughts and ideas. If you set your standards high, the only person you have to impress is yourself. Everyone else will already have cause to admire you.

Has anyone ever seen a junk pile look better by piling more junk on it? When General Jones retired as the supreme allied commander of NATO, he was offered a series of high-level jobs. He never compromised his principles whether in the military or in civilian life.

My life has been blessed by examples of leaders unwilling to bend no matter which way the wind blew or how hard. These lessons aren't taken from psychology lectures I read in a book. From my mother and grandmother to men like Ross Rosborough, Butch Morgan, Wes Fox, and General Jones, I've witnessed first hand the power and dignity that comes from impressing yourself first.

Rely on Intelligence over Emotion: Lessons in Black and White

I WAS ONLY FIVE YEARS old when my grandfather, Sherman, took to a bed in the living room of our house. He was dying of cancer and the year was 1957, a year that means something to African-Americans in the south, particularly those living in Arkansas.

He was tall and dark and looked like the actor Don Cheadle. He was known as Smokey, partly because of his deeply dark skin and partly, no doubt, because of his affinity for late-night activities. He loved the liquor and he liked to gamble a little, too, sometimes a little too much.

At one point our house was set to go into foreclosure, so my grandmother, Ida, went down to the bank to straighten things out. From that moment on, the bank dealt exclusively with Ida. The banker in charge, who was a white man, tried to convince her to put the property deed in her own name because he no longer had any business confidence in my grandfather. But like everyone else in town, he knew and respected my grandmother. For whatever reason, the only thing she ever changed was the person making the monthly payment. And to this day the deed for Helm Street shows the name of Sherman McMichael because that's the way she wanted it.

From what I remember from those early years, my grandmother never knew how much Smokey was going to drink or how much he was going to gamble, which meant she never knew exactly how much money would be coming home each week.

Yet there he lay on a bed she had prepared for him in the living room of our home in our all-African-American neighborhood. Ida would look after him in the morning, then she'd walk the mile or more to work at Hot Springs High School. At lunchtime, she'd walk the same route back home, get Smokey fed, and then walk back again. She made that trip and tended to that man every day until he died.

My grandmother never abandoned her husband despite his big-city lifestyle, and neither did his friends, most of whom were white men.

What I remember most was all the people who came by the house every day: ten to twenty people would stop to see how my grandfather was doing. There were white men with businesses, men who worked with Smokey at the best garage in town, men who wore suits, and men who carried lunch boxes. There were black men, too.

Even though segregation was the order of the day, we had white neighbors just beyond our backyard fence. Some rules were understood and went unchallenged. But everybody mixed when they came through our front door, the same way they did around town. All these people, black and white, were like family to us, and they never did a thing to make us feel otherwise.

I was named after my great-grandfather, Smokey's father, Alford. He worked in a mattress factory, but he also was involved in the city business. He is credited with helping bring the Oaklawn Park horse racing track to Hot Springs, though he died a day before the track opened.

That's one reason my grandparents had so much respect within the community—and it's why color never was an issue in our house. We knew we were black, no one had to tell us that. But we never felt any less—nor were we made to feel less— than anyone else.

When my grandmother moved to Hot Springs from North Little Rock in the early 1930s, she carried herself with a dignity apparent to people who didn't even know her. My grandfather, Smokey, was a master mechanic and everyone in town knew that, too. He and my grandmother moved to Detroit briefly when my mother was a young girl, and Smokey worked for General Motors before deciding to come back to Hot Springs.

In September of 1957, President Dwight Eisenhower sent troops from the Army's 101st Airborne Division into Little Rock, just fifty-two miles away. Arkansas governor Orval Faubus had threatened to prevent nine African-American students, the Little Rock Nine as they became known, from entering previously all-white Central High School. Though it was more than three years after the Supreme Court ruled segregated schools unconstitutional in *Brown v. Board of Education,* nothing had changed yet in Little Rock or Hot Springs.

Although I didn't go to school with a white person until 1968 when I was sixteen years old and a junior in high school, the intensity of the racial discourse that blew through the rest of the country never made its way into Hot Springs, not even as the issue threatened to boil over in Little Rock. And it sure didn't have a chance in our house.

We were brought up to respect all people whom we could count on, whose values and character reflected those of our grandmother. We weren't color blind, but the color of one's skin wasn't the deciding factor in how we interacted with folks. There wasn't any room for that kind of exclusionary thinking in a house where everyone had to work just to survive.

We were cognizant of race, and we knew there were different rules for us, but we were taught to understand those rules so we could withstand them. It was wrong for us to *think* we were less, but it was even more wrong to *believe* we were less.

My mother and Grandma Ida constantly reminded us that we were McMichaels. That was how we were taught to define ourselves first, not by a color, a job, or even a neighborhood. That lesson was a key one and reflected our experience because we saw how our grandparents were treated, and we had white people who were important to us in our lives.

"The McMichaels are people who rise to the occasion," we were told, "people who endure and move forward with pride and dignity."

The issue of race was packaged without any hint of inferiority. Family superceded skin color, and those old-fashioned values delivered at the dinner table made it next to impossible for us to value people on the basis of appearance. Now that I think about it, my grandmother wasn't teaching us about race as much as she was helping us understand how to deal with larger societal issues over which we had no control. We were learning to use our intelligence and sense of integrity to overcome other people's prejudices that more often than not were based purely on emotion.

We were never taught to think badly of anyone because of how they looked or because they could go into the King Kong Restaurant through the front door, while we had to order our cheeseburgers at the back window.

Mr. Bob, who ran the liquor store, and Mr. Charlie, who worked with my grandfather at Lions filling station, were white, to name only two, and were extensions of our family. It never occurred to us to hate anyone, because we had white friends.

My grandparents' reputation extended beyond our neighborhood and into the rest of the city. They didn't garner that respect by having an attitude that caused tension or by bowing their heads or bringing a slave-like mentality to their interactions with white people. They carried themselves with dignity and they treated everyone the same way.

What they gave is what they got in return, and it had nothing to do with color.

I didn't realize how they were perceived until I started working outside our neighborhood. When people found out I was Ida and Smokey's grandson, that carried weight.

Now it wasn't like we didn't suffer from segregation and later with integration. Color made a difference even in Hot Springs. But we endured because there was positive leadership in our house. We knew the difference between what we could control and what we couldn't. Mostly we understood that we couldn't make value judgments on people based on a factor over which they themselves had no control—the color of their skin or the hair on their head or the weight on their bones.

I was twelve years old when the Civil Rights Act of 1964 was passed on July 2, 1964. That act became law under the Commerce Clause that, among other things, outlawed discrimination in public facilities.

I may be off a day or two, but as I remember it, the very next day we could go into what had been the white movie theaters. At the time, there were three theaters in town. The Paramount was exclusively white, the Central and the Malco Theaters were for everyone. Until the Civil Rights Act, we were only allowed into the Paramount if we were there to clean the place.

I remember going to the Malco to see Westerns. African-Americans had to go in through the side door, which was down near many of the black businesses, and we had to head straight into the balcony. White people could enter on Central Avenue through the front door. The main floor was reserved for them. The irony is that once we could sit down on the main level with all the white people we realized the best seats in the house were in the balcony.

A few years later, even as major American cities erupted in violence, first with the assassination of Dr. King on April 4, 1968, at the Lorraine Motel in Memphis, and then two months later with the assassination of Senator Robert F. Kennedy in Los Angeles just after midnight on June 5, and three days before James Earl Ray was arrested for the murder of Dr. King, our lives did not buckle under the social strain.

When we went to school the day after Dr. King's death, the emotion that fueled riots in larger cities presented itself differently in Hot Springs. We had two white teachers at our school, Langston High, and not a single white student. One of those white teachers was Miss Johnson, and I remember her talking us through what had happened. There was anger, but the dominant feeling was of sadness and loss. It was the kind of pain that came with the passing of a revered family member, someone very close who had gone too soon. There were students who were very upset, including a few girls who cried in anguish.

"They killed our king," one of them said. "They killed our president."

The way Miss Johnson talked to us that day was memorable to me because it provided insight into the way race was dealt with in Hot Springs. Here was a white woman talking to a classroom full of black kids in a high school with two white faces, one of them hers. She handled it beautifully.

"There are bad people in the world who can and will do bad things to us, but you don't have to destroy yourself in the process of dealing with their evil," she said. "You can rise above those people. You can control your own lives. Don't let the actions of evil people affect who you are or who you can become."

Regardless of what happened elsewhere, there was never a desire to grab baseball bats in our community and destroy things that had nothing to do with the evil that had happened in Memphis, just 180 miles away. The riots that broke out in other cities were the result of the lid coming off tensions that already existed. We didn't have that level of tension in Hot Springs, which is not to say it was completely absent, either. It just wasn't of a depth that made anyone consider violence as a reasonable response.

In the seven days that followed Dr. King's murder, a shoot-out in California between Oakland police and the Black Panthers resulted in the death of a seventeen-year-old named Bobby Hutton. President Lyndon Johnson signed the Civil Rights Act of 1968, a follow-up to the 1964 law, designed to eliminate housing discrimination and protect civil rights workers. Later that same month, students protesting the Vietnam War shut down Columbia University in New York City.

I'll never know whether any of those events impacted my brother Sherman's decision to quit high school and join the Marine Corps. If they did, he never spoke of it and I never asked him. In the fall of that year, in a newly built Hot Springs High School outside of town, integration finally came to Hot Springs. Despite the societal spasms being felt elsewhere, I don't recall anything particularly noteworthy about the experience of sitting in the same classroom with white kids.

For one thing, I knew a lot of them. The children of all those doctors for whom my mother worked knew us. We had played together. It wasn't like I had been bussed in from out of town to suddenly interact with these kids. No one was loading up kids from another town and bussing them into an all-white school. We grew up together. Most of us knew one another. Now, there were incidents, nothing violent, but enough to make everyone understand the times were changing.

Through it all, we never felt like we had to keep our heads down, or stay in the house. We had our block parties. Blacks continued to go to one church, whites to another. But as far we knew, we all prayed to the same God.

I'm thankful I lived in those times, but I'm most thankful I lived in those times the way I did. I'm thankful I didn't have to grow up in other parts of the United States, in the major cities where the tension was dramatically different than it was in Hot Springs. That's not to say it was easy, or without hardship. You couldn't avoid the fact that you were black any more than you could avoid the fact that white people had their own neighborhoods and lived by different rules.

But it took me less than a week in the Marine Corps to understand just how different my experience had been versus those of other African-American Marines, particularly those from cities like Detroit, Chicago, New York, and Los Angeles. Luckily, I had been counseled all those years at home to let my intelligence rule when confronted with prejudice and hateful emotion.

ONE OF THE FIRST lessons you are taught in the Marine Corps is that everyone is the same. That kind of mental mind shaping is part of what is called the "teardown process" in boot camp. It might just as well be called a toxin removal process. Whatever negative thoughts, behaviors, habits, or prejudices you arrive with are dealt with every minute of every day. Those beliefs or practices are not tolerated and systems are in place to remind you of that fact.

But when we went on liberty, and no one was around to closely monitor or police everyone's behavior, those toxic attitudes were able to roll out in full view.

My best friend in boot camp was Toby Hawkins, a six foot one, hundred-and-sixty-pound white boy from Mountain View, Oklahoma. You couldn't get more rural than that. But Toby was the gentlest person in the world, the kind of person you wanted to be your friend. I didn't see Toby as a white boy. I saw him as a good person I wanted to be around. We both looked like babies and yet, within eighteen months, we were sergeants out together on liberty. Toby made sergeant before I did because he received an accelerated, or meritorious, promotion. We were on the same track and we worked together to make sure we stayed that way.

But that track is where I learned the true meaning of racial words and phrases like "Uncle Tom," "Oreo," and a host of others. I remember thinking, *What are you talking about?*

The other black Marines couldn't understand how I could be hanging out with a white guy and not them.

I didn't wear the black bands made of boot laces around my wrists to signify a silent protest of the Vietnam War as well as what the rest of society stood for. I didn't join in on the "dapping," a handshake the black Marines brought back from the war. I made the decision I wasn't going to curry favor by joining that mind-set, which at its core was designed to separate one group from another while perpetuating racial disharmony. I understood where those Marines were coming from, but I saw no upside to their approach.

Were there white officers who didn't like some of us precisely because of our skin color? There's no question about that. In fact, there were few black officers anywhere in the Marine Corps in 1970. But I also recognized how counterproductive it was to separate myself in the name of fighting the system. We weren't going to change anything by defying the system, particularly when it was managed exclusively by people who looked different than we did. We didn't have the power to change a thing. So who won and who lost in that equation?

I was far from a genius, but I knew the answer to that question.

If I wanted to advance into leadership positions where I could influence change, then I had to do what the system demanded of me. Some people in the military were far from color-blind, but the system itself disregarded color when it came to performance. The demands were the same for every person: male, female, black, white, Hispanic, or otherwise.

"I don't dap and I don't separate myself from other Marines," I said one day after entering the mess hall and being invited to sit at an all-black table.

"What do you mean, you don't dap?" an African-American soldier asked. "What's wrong with you?"

Once I made the decision I wasn't going to buy into the existing racial paradigm, I traveled my own path. It was a very straightforward decision for me. I could have decided to go over to a separate table with those guys and talk about how bad white people were, create a lot of havoc, and get into trouble. Or, I could follow the rules and regulations and compete to be the best.

I developed a very simple approach. I would succeed or fail solely on the merits of my own performance, nothing more or less. Those other guys might have made their point, but a lot of them either ended up in the brig or they were kicked out of the military. It wasn't a very difficult decision. But it wasn't a rose-covered path, either.

I understood and appreciated the situation we were in. Many of the black Marines had either been to Vietnam or they had come from very difficult and racially charged environments as civilians. Suddenly they were reporting to officers, most of whom were white, and in many cases being yelled at, treated poorly, and pushed to perform day in and day out. I can appreciate that wasn't easy for them psychologically because it wasn't easy for me, either.

At the same time, we all had a very clear choice. Fight the system and lose, or work within the system and remove any questions by performing at the highest possible level.

It's what I've always called "I over E," intelligence over emotion. Emotions were raw in those days, and anyone with even the slightest empathy could understand why. But it was a losing proposition, and to me a clear sign of weakness, to give in to those emotions when the outcome was crystal clear. No one could win taking that route. The choices were very limited, but the right one—to use my intelligence—was obvious.

At times, I was cursed or screamed at even when I knew my superior was wrong. Was that behavior directed at me because of the color of my skin? I don't know, but it was certainly within the realm of possibility at that time. I could read. I knew what the rules were. Was this man too stupid to understand that I was right and he was wrong? Rather than debate with someone like that, I chose to move past him by being even better.

When the platoon sergeant wanted to be a hero at my expense, he was really just setting himself up for failure. I wasn't going to allow that toxicity to affect me to the point that I became hateful or abusive. There is value in that old saying, "This too will pass." It usually does, but it's how you come out the other side that matters. I decided to treat disagreements or injustices just as I dealt with the issue of race. I could buy into the idea I had been wronged and allow it to affect my performance, or I could refuse to embrace excuses and move on.

WHEN I ENTERED THE Marine Corps, I didn't buy into the "white people are holding us down" angle. That wouldn't have washed in my house. Now, there were no doubt people in my community who held those views, but that wasn't an option in my family. That was an excuse. And excuses were not tolerated as far as my mother and grandmother were concerned. I had no excuse for not doing my absolute best at all times, because I had a choice, a choice over which I had total control. I could choose to follow every step and perform at my highest possible level, or I could choose to take shortcuts and settle for something less than excellence. So when I heard discussions about how white people had taken this or that away from these guys, it didn't compute for me.

If you never had a job, how did a white person take it away?

Maybe your attitude was so negative you didn't give anyone a chance to provide a job.

I needed a job. I valued a job. I wanted to bring an attitude to the table that signaled to those in charge that investing in me was worthwhile. But I had no chance of convincing anyone of that if I came in saying, "You white people are holding me back" or "You're taking advantage of me."

If someone didn't like me because of something as shallow as my skin color, then they didn't know me. I wanted to penetrate that ignorance. I knew those feelings existed because I saw them all around me, but it wasn't until I joined the military that those thoughts hit me in the face.

I had two good, solid years at an integrated high school. I had never experienced someone telling me they didn't like me because I was black. Now, all of a sudden, these little cells or groups thought it was okay to blatantly tell people what they thought of them based almost exclusively on color. And it wasn't just white people. African-Americans were doing it, too. Both groups did it and one was just as ignorant as the other.

"Are you kidding me?" I said to one of them. "These are the same people we play football with. These are the same guys we went through boot camp with. Now you can be open about the fact you don't like them because you can form a little group that thinks like you?"

Sure white people made some rules that slowed down my progress, but no one denied my ability to succeed. If the Marine Corps was a racist institution, then how did I advance so quickly? How did I advance at all? Who wrote my fitness reports, the evaluations that allowed me to compete at the highest level against all the other Marines, most of whom were white? Few black officers were writing those reports in those days. In my entire thirty-six-year career I only had one fitness report written by an African-American, and that was Major Butch Morgan.

That's not to say it wasn't hard, or that I was spared the ignorance of racism. In fact, I saw it in just about every form it could be expressed, and neither my rank nor my accomplishments was enough to eliminate those experiences.

I had a long list of firsts before I became the first African-American

Sergeant Major of the Marine Corps. I was the first African-American to lead a Marine detachment at the United States embassy in Copenhagen, Denmark, in 1979. The Danes were well aware of the racial strife in the United States, so when I arrived, they were surprised to say the least.

"How can you tell these guys what to do?" I was asked. "They aren't going to listen to you. You're black."

"Yes, that's true," I said. "But they're colored too, just like you. I'm colored black and you're colored white so we're all colored. And besides, in the United States military, rank outshines color whether it's white, black, or brown."

Then two years later, in 1981, I left Denmark and returned to Quantico to serve as one of the first, if not the first black instructor in the history of the Embassy School, which was established in 1947. On my first day back at Quantico, I stuck my head into a room where a number of other instructors were hanging out.

"Where is the chief instructor?" I asked.

"Students go down the hall to the right," came the answer. They couldn't believe I was anything more than a student, a candidate for embassy duty, even though I had previously been DET Commander in Denmark. It never occurred to any of them because of my skin color that I might be their equal.

I knew then that the Embassy School this time around, as an instructor instead of as a student, wasn't going to be as easy as I wanted it to be. Once more, I chose to take it as an opportunity to rise above the prevailing mind-set. I went in and made good friends who remain close to this day.

One day, all the instructors went to lunch at a restaurant in town. The waitresses were white. They were serving us, and all of us were talking to them. We were just being polite, nothing more than that. When we got back to the base, the chief instructor called me into his office.

"In my religion," he said to me, "there is no gray."

"Okay," I said. "What does that mean?"

"Well, today we went to lunch and you were talking to the waitresses."

"Everybody was talking to them."

"Yes, but you talked to them, too. In my religion there is no gray."

"I heard you the first time, but I don't understand what you mean."

"In my religion you are either black or you are white, but there is no in between."

This was 1981, and he was a master sergeant, my superior.

RACE DID COME OVERTLY into play at that time, though it was outside of the military. My daughter, Portia, had been born abroad on January 11, 1980, and so we needed to find a babysitter once we were back in Virginia. We did find a woman we thought would be good, but almost immediately we started to notice little bruises on Portia when we brought her home at the end of the day. On the third day, convinced they were not the result of normal play activity, my wife, Rita, confronted the babysitter. Thank God the woman was honest about her prejudice.

"I can't keep your child any more," she said. "I don't babysit black kids."

Rita was horrified. How had we missed the signs? She couldn't imagine anyone having such malice for our little girl. But by then, I'd been exposed to the full menu of racial bias. So I was able to see the situation from a different angle. Yes, it was repulsive to think anyone could have such hateful feelings for—much less purposely abuse—a child because of the color of her skin. But at least we found out quickly. A lot of people might keep their prejudice out of view. So I was glad we were free of this woman. Her ugliness was front and center, and we were better off for knowing it.

Once again for me, I over E allowed me to see the ignorance of her ways and move past it.

No matter what you think about yourself, somebody is always going to have another opinion—and sometimes it may be based on the color of your skin. But if you worry about what others think, rather than focus on what you need to be doing, you will set yourself up to fail.

I have never involved myself with trying to change what people think of me, especially on the basis of race, because I don't have the time or the space in my life to concentrate on convincing them of their wrong-headedness. I know that if I tried, then I'd never have a life of my own.

Instead I let my intelligence rule on this issue. I rely on I over E, intelligence over emotion, to guide me in my personal and professional life.

5

Prepare So You Can Prosper: ESP— Establish, Streamline, Prioritize

LEARNING THE POWER OF preparation started early in my life. I was nothing if not organized. If I hadn't figured out how to establish what I needed to get done, streamline the process, and prioritize my actions (what I now call "ESP"), I never could have finished all my house chores and still found time for homework, fun, and an outside job. Preparation was as much about performance as it was survival when I was growing up.

I didn't realize it then, but the "one penny at a time" philosophy I employed in the Marine Corps was a part of my life even as a child. Pennies make dollars. I believe in this concept not only in finance but in life. You have to have a penny's worth of effort invested today if you want to have a dollar's worth of success three months down the line.

We have become a culture focused on the dollar at the expense of the investment process. A "something for nothing" mentality has invaded our collective mind-set. From the lottery to the stock market and real estate bubbles to frivolous lawsuits, we accept the notion that the ends—the dollars—justify the means. Along the way, we've lost sight of the day-to-day, step-by-step processes necessary to move us ahead.

And yet people in general don't appear to be as happy as I was as a child. Why? Because it's very difficult to find true joy from something that demands very little from us. I know we were happier back then in my family on a day-to-day basis than a whole lot of kids whose parents gave them everything.

I believe the value of the item—which is different than the cost—decreases relative to the effort invested. If dollars truly did grow on trees, no one would want them. Money has an unusual psychological component that can't be dismissed. We all feel better about our successes when our effort matches the reward.

At that time, life to me was about efficiency and simplification. Demands were placed on all of us all the time in my house. From taking care of the inside of the house to the animals and gardens on the outside to making sure school work was in order, we had a lot going on. So I instinctively created systems or processes that allowed me to execute my chores quickly without skipping a step. Any lapse in judgment always had the potential of ending in a meeting between my behind and my mother's hand.

I had to organize my day and create a system for doing chores, so I had time to earn money for things important to me. Everyone had to work hard in our house, and none of us were afraid of it. But I discovered that if I planned ahead, things that might normally have been out of my economic reach were attainable. As a result, the ability to organize myself became second nature.

When I was about nine years old, I really wanted a bike. I thought about saving what little money I made doing odd jobs around the neighborhood. I also thought about saving most of my lunch money every day. But when I added those two ideas together, I ended up broke, hungry, and still without a bike. I couldn't ask my mother or grandmother because I understood how tightly they managed the family budget. So that left Blue Horses.

Blue Horses were easy to find in Hot Springs in the late 1950s and early 1960s. If you went to school, you had a Blue Horse Notebook made by the Montag Brothers Paper Company in Atlanta. These notebooks sold for a dime apiece. On the cover was the company's trademark, the blue head of a horse framed by a thin-lined box with a white picket fence in the background.

The Montag Brothers had a creative marketing department focused on brand loyalty. The company worked with all the schools to sell the notebooks to children and their parents with two clever hooks.

First, the schools had a chance to win a small cash prize based on how many notebooks and paper packets were sold. Second, children were enticed to clip and save Blue Horses for "50,000 Prizes For All You Lucky Boys And Girls," as one wrapper stated.

But to get enough Blue Horses for a bike, I needed a plan.

I certainly wasn't going to embarrass myself by jumping into garbage bins in front of everyone at school looking for Blue Horses. So I volunteered to empty the garbage pail every day for my teachers, which had the added benefit of making a positive impression on them. I also walked a mile back to school on Saturdays because that's when the week's garbage was taken out to the large bins. But in our elementary school, there weren't many notebooks to be found because there weren't that many to start with. We wrote on both sides of each sheet, and you didn't throw a notebook away until every last inch of paper had been used. I needed a whole lot of Blue Horses, hundreds of them.

Time for Plan B. I was just old enough to help my grandmother clean classrooms on the fourth floor of Hot Springs High School. Now those kids didn't need Blue Horses. Most of them already had bikes. Not only that, but they threw away a lot of notebooks—many with only one side of the paper used. I couldn't believe that. So I never had even the slightest problem reaching into the trash to pull out those Blue Horses.

"Thank you very much," I remember thinking each time I picked one up.

My grandmother never wavered when it came to the work ethic. If one of us wanted something, she'd find a way to make us earn it. She would help out, but only if you were willing to do your part. Make a deposit, take a withdrawal. Another one of those dinner table values. So my grandmother made me a deal.

"If you come help me after school, whatever notebooks you find are yours. You keep those Blue Horses for yourself. I'll look for them the rest of the day, but whatever I find will be split between you and your brother."

The plan worked perfectly because my grandmother always gave me more than Sherman. I thought I was being rewarded for my hard work. She knew Sherman already had a bike. It took a while, but eventually I came up with enough Blue Horses to get my first, brand new bike.

In our town, the driver of any delivery truck, just like the men who brought the groceries from Cooley's, carried whatever you ordered right up to the front door. I was walking home from school down Helm Street when I saw the big, brown truck. I couldn't believe it. It was in front of *my* house. In that moment, I could have outrun Carl Lewis in a hundred-yard dash. I ran faster than I had ever run before, and I didn't stop until I reached the front steps. The driver opened up the back of the truck, grabbed the big box, and brought it up our steps. He wasn't even back down when I was tearing that box open. I stayed there until I had my bicycle put together. It was red. And it was beautiful.

THE DAILY DEMANDS THAT came with growing up in our house led me to develop a disciplined, systematic way of organizing just about everything in my life. I knew I wasn't smart enough to get everything done and still have time to play if I didn't figure out a way to do it all efficiently.

Initially, I was motivated to be organized to avoid my mother's fury. Later on, it became a way of life, a process to eliminate confusion. For example, I always put my shoes in exactly the same place near my bed. I did the same with the clothes I planned to wear the next day. I wanted to be able to find everything I needed even in the dark. And I could.

Being well organized has helped me prosper throughout my military career. When I became sergeant major of Manpower Reserve Affairs in 1998, it served me especially well.

To this day I call my system ESP:

Establish what you want to achieve.

Streamline the process.

Prioritize your actions.

ONE OF THE MOST important organizational operations we executed during my time at Manpower was moving the Marine Corps headquarters south from Washington to the Marine base at Quantico in northern Virginia. It was a massive undertaking with understandable resistance.

Some of the civilians working at Marine headquarters had been there for twenty years or more. They lived in that area because of those jobs, and their commutes to the office were convenient and well rehearsed.

We also had files in the hundreds of thousands going back decades, the vast majority of which had yet to be computerized in any meaningful way. If someone called with a question about Vietnam, then someone else had to dig into a paper file to find the answer. We needed to relocate and modernize our data retrieval.

Like any good leader, Lt. General Carol Mutter, who was in charge of Manpower, didn't just send out a letter or dictate change from her office. She went out and "socialized" the issue. The more information about the relocation she could provide effectively early on, the easier it would be to eliminate resisters.

We knew many people were entrenched in keeping the status quo, not just in Washington but in Quantico as well. Many at the base in Virginia didn't want an influx of new workers coming down from Washington to mess up their traffic patterns and take all the parking spaces. Even the Military Police (MP) at Quantico worried about all the new people they would have to watch over.

Lt. General Mutter put together a slide show she presented around the Marine Corps. The first talk was in a gymnasium at Henderson Hall in Arlington, Virginia. As she talked about the move, I scanned the audience to see the reaction. I wasn't sure that all of them were listening even though every one of them needed the information.

Lt. General Mutter discussed housing, schools for the children, everything a Marine involved in the move would have to know. She laid it all out clearly. But the presentation was lacking a hook to catch the Marines, to draw them in and get them on board. She needed something to pull them out of the bleachers and into the palm of her hand.

A couple of days later we traveled to California, where she was scheduled to present her talk to another group of Marines.

"You are going to deliver that lecture again tomorrow?" I asked.

"Yes."

"Wow, wait until they hear about your ESP."

"My ESP? What do you mean, Sergeant Major?"

"That's what you talk about—eliminating, streamlining, and prioritizing. To me, that's ESP. That's what those Marines need to know. You are telling them how to have ESP."

The next day she had them from the opening slide.

"Yesterday, the sergeant major told me I had ESP," she said. "So today I want to share my ESP with you."

This time she had them hooked. She talked about eliminating useless paperwork, scanning files into the computer, then downloading them onto discs. Those Marines were tuned into every fact.

The point is, she needed that honest feedback for the program to really succeed. And that required me to listen and watch. In the Marine Corps, there are two places for generals to get honest feedback—from their sergeant major or the chaplain. I have had to have the intestinal fortitude to share information honestly, even when that might not be what my boss wanted to hear.

I've prepared for that task by learning everything I can about the person I report to. Not to impress that person, but to be better able to lend support. It is as important to know who I am working for as it is for me to know the people I lead. In this case, for example, I knew that when Lt. General Mutter came into the office every morning, she was bombarded by various requests. She was in a transmitting mode throughout most of the day because she had to address immediate needs. She wasn't usually receptive to new ideas until later in the day when things calmed down. She also had a great intellect and could analyze and organize complex ideas very quickly. I definitely sharpened my organizational skills under her tutelage.

I HAVE USED ESP throughout my career to help me hone my skills, such as public speaking. By the time I became Sergeant Major of the Marine Corps in 1999, General Jones routinely shared public speaking responsibilities with me. More than once, I found myself sitting out in the audience at a table full of people waiting for General Jones to speak, only to have all eyes suddenly turn on me.

"I am honored to be here," the general said at one function at a naval training facility in Pensacola, Florida. "And tonight we will all have the privilege of listening to the fourteenth Sergeant Major of the Marines Corps, Sergeant Major McMichael."

So I wasn't shocked when a member of General Jones's staff came into my office at the Pentagon in July 2001. I had been Sergeant Major of the Marine Corps for almost exactly two years at this point. The staff person told me the general wanted me to speak at an important ceremony we were to attend that week. I assumed General Jones wouldn't be able to make the event, which I was surprised by given the Marines being honored. I went down to his office as requested to find out the specifics.

"You want me to speak at the ceremony, General?"

"Yes, Sergeant Major. Could you do that?"

"Not a problem, sir."

The Congressional Gold Medal ceremony to honor the Navajo Code Talkers was to take place in the Capitol Rotunda. President Bush was going to present Gold Medals to the first twenty-nine Navajo Code Talkers in a historic event. The standing-room-only audience would include members of Congress, the Marine Corps leadership, Code Talker family members, and other dignitaries.

Every Marine knows the story. More than 400 Code Talkers served in all six Marine divisions between 1942 and 1945 during World War II. They are credited with saving countless lives by helping to bring the war to an end. According to the Navajo Code Talkers Association, their primary job was to transmit details on troop movement, tactics, orders, and other vital battlefield information via telegraph and radio in their native dialect.

The Japanese were never able to crack the code. First, the system was much faster than Morse code, which could take hours. The Navajos transmitted messages in minutes. Second, the Code Talkers Association notes that fewer than thirty non-Navajo speakers understood the Navajo's unwritten language at the time. The complexity of the language and its almost completely isolated usage made it effectively incomprehensible even to those who had heard it spoken. The strategic advantage was so great that the code wasn't declassified by the Department of Defense until 1968, more than twenty years after the war. Without the efforts of these men the Marines might never have taken Iwo Jima.

On the day of the ceremony I arrived in my dress blues all squared away. The next thing I knew, General Jones walked in. I was thinking, *What are you doing here?*

"You have a big job. You have something important to do here today."

"No, sir."

I saw an expression of concern come over his face.

"You are speaking, right?"

"Oh, yes, sir, I'm speaking. But it's no big deal."

I was trying to stay calm and ready because I never speak using notes of any kind. We headed into the Rotunda and up to the stage where all the congressmen and senators were seated along with the Navajo Code Talkers. One by one, the politicians pulled out their three-ring binders where their speeches had been prepared and placed, usually by a staff member.

When it was my turn, I walked to the podium empty handed. I thanked everyone on the platform and began speaking about the Navajo Code Talkers. I never referred to them as Native Americans. I referred to them as United States Marines who provided the country with a language that made possible what Tom Brokaw has called the "The Greatest Generation." Everyone else before me had talked about how the country had forgotten about these men. My speech was a little different. I spoke about a grateful nation. Recognition might have been long coming, but it had never been forgotten. Their contributions to our freedoms and democracy were evident by the way we live today.

I didn't really get emotional, but I was talking from my heart about these men and what they did for the United States of America.

"Today our great nation takes time to say 'thank you' to some of America's greatest heroes. Our country adds to its legacy and its history because of these great Americans who grace the stage today. I can only imagine the hardships they endured in performing their duties. But these Marines were instrumental in allowing us to have the freedom that we enjoy.

"The recognition they receive today is most deeply and honorably deserved. I know that some would say recognition is long overdue, but I submit to you that a ceremony of this nature is evidence that a great nation never forgets, and never fails to say 'thank you' to the great men and women that serve in uniform. These Marines who served as code talkers were the majestic force of the South Pacific. These are the men who knew how to deliver a code that could not be broken by any enemy.

"Theirs is a contribution all Americans should know and remember. Today we embrace that memory and hold it with the pride and the dignity that it deserves. Their contribution to this country is part of the fiber of what we call the greatest generation. I can only think of the original twenty-nine Code Talkers who answered our country when it called for a few good men to serve and protect. As you receive your Gold Medal today, keep it close to your heart.

"It should be gold and it should shine bright. But I will say to you that it will never shine so bright as to outshine the respect, honor, and the dignity that America has for your contributions. I have struggled trying to find the right words to say 'thank you.' As you know, it's not customary for Marines to say what they feel, but I offer to you two words that I place on silver platter for you today. Those two words are *Semper Fidelis.* So I say to you, *Semper Fidelis,* Navajo Code Talkers. *Semper Fidelis,* my fellow Marines. *Semper Fidelis,* my fellow Americans. God bless you and God bless America."

Semper Fidelis, the Marine Corps motto, is Latin for "Always Faithful." When I finished, the audience erupted.

I left the podium as then Speaker of the House Dennis Hastert came up to introduce President Bush. The audience wouldn't sit down. They gave me a standing ovation and the Speaker had to wait until they finished. In my mind, I had only done what General Jones had asked me to do. That's the way Marines operate.

That night we had a ceremony at Eighth Avenue and I Street at the Marine Corps Barracks in Washington, D.C., a hallmark of the Marine Corps. The barracks has a large parade field, and anything of importance that involves the Marine Corps is held there. It's also where the commandant lives.

"Today I had the pleasure of hearing one of the greatest speeches I've ever heard," General Jones told the audience.

Then later, a former commandant, General P. X. Kelly, said, "I've heard a lot of people speak and I've been to a lot of events, but that was the best speech I've ever heard."

Of course I was flattered. But it also made me feel good to know that a lifetime of training myself to always be prepared had once again paid off. With only a few days notice, I had been able to efficiently gather my thoughts about these great men. The core of the speech was the same one I had delivered hundreds of times before and since.

I KNOW WHAT I believe and I try hard to live by those values every single day. It makes no difference to me whether I am talking to at-risk kids in Harlem or speaking in front of the president of the United

States. My message is essentially the same. I might choose different words so the two groups can grasp my message, but I'm not selling anything I haven't already bought into and used as a foundation in my own life. I was prepared for that moment, that speech, and dozens of others like it over the years because I have made preparation part of who I am. That confidence took away the pressure. By speaking from my heart rather than from someone else's, I always stay true to myself.

I have always found comfort in the kind of processes and systems that inform preparation. It has allowed me to focus on the smaller details, the ones that can separate the good from the great. This has been true throughout my career.

One of my very first jobs in the Marine Corps was standing guard at the Naval Communications base in 1971 in the middle of pineapple fields on the island of Oahu. Our country was still at war and so was the culture.

The Weather Underground claimed responsibility for exploding a bomb in a men's room inside the Capitol that March. Later that month, Army Lieutenant William Calley was found guilty in the My Lai massacre trial. Then, on April 24, 1971, 500,000 people marched against the war in Washington, D.C., with another 125,000 marching in protest in San Francisco. By June, the *New York Times* had started publishing the "Pentagon Papers." Guard duty was serious business.

I wanted to be sure I had a system down for how to do my job so well that I could perform it automatically, without thought. So when I returned to my room at the end of every day I took off my cover, or hat, and placed it in the same spot every time. My lanyard, the cord that went around my body and connected me to my weapon, went in its place. I created a specific place for every piece of my uniform, and I never varied the routine.

Once I laid out my uniform and redressed in civilian clothes, I headed straight to the dining hall. I spent a set amount of time eating before I went back to my room to prepare for guard duty the next day.

I never had a problem relaxing because I always knew everything that needed to be done had already been done. I never spent one restless night thinking:

I have to shine my shoes.
I have to wash my white gear.
I have to shine my cover.
I have to shine my brass.

And I never put fun ahead of getting my preparation done because I knew whatever enjoyment I hoped to have would be relative. Once again, my habits came from my childhood. I had to do my chores and get my homework done before I could go out and play.

It might sound as if I was a robot. But what I really did was create freedom and eliminate stress in my personal life. I was able to be completely in the moment because there wasn't anywhere else for me to be. Other guys had those same obligations, but by the time they made it back to the room after dinner and fun, they were fatigued. Always being prepared is one of those small details that has allowed me to succeed.

It's also a key principle to effective leadership. By being prepared, I was able to be fully committed to the present moment rather than distracted by what I yet had to do.

Preparing in advance to perform has always helped create space between me and those I competed against. I knew I didn't have enough natural ability to be lazy. Discipline and routine allowed me to compete against people who were far better than me. But they never knew that, because I produced at the same level consistently. As far as they knew, I was as blessed as they were.

That is an important psychological advantage in an environment as competitive as the United States Marine Corps. In that respect, climbing the corporate ladder has nothing on the Marine Corps. The process of elimination starts early and it never ends. It is a constant and relentless methodology designed to ensure only the best leaders survive. People can slip through for a while, but eventually the system is going to expose them.

In the Marine Corps, that system is operational from the first day of boot camp until your last day in uniform. Every step is a test designed to weed out the weak so the strong can continue moving ahead.

Marine Security Guard School (MSG) is an excellent example of this weeding process at work. The leadership training course takes place at Quantico, in Virginia, and it is different from virtually all other training cycles in the Marine Corps. As much as 75 percent of this program is State Department specific, dealing with everything from protocol logistics to protecting classified information. You are taught how to conduct business on a post, how to check passports, and sign visitors into and out of an embassy. You learn how to call in a bomb threat, ways to pick up on the nuances of a voice over the phone to tell whether the caller is foreign, local, male, or female. Only 25 percent of the program deals with the Marine Corps. You are tested on every element of training with a unique twist.

As a senior NCO in the spring of 1979, I was given ten Marines junior to me. They became my detachment throughout the training cycle. In other words, I was the leader of the group. I was not, however, evaluated independent of the group. My success was determined by the success of the unit. If I tested perfectly and the rest of the group tested mediocre, then I failed. The score of every person in the unit in every section—physical fitness, inspection, morning cleanup, subject tests—carried the same weight.

The leadership proposition was simple: Were you capable of leading a group of people in a way that raised the performance of the entire unit?

Our unit score on that day's subject determined how we measured up against all the other detachments in that cycle.

Once again, I needed a plan of attack. As with everything else in the Marine Corps, competition spiced the process. I could have told

My mother, Rosa, and I in the summer of 1975. (Private Collection)

Rita and I with our son-in-law, Darren Blunt, and our daughter, Portia, at the Marine Corps Law Enforcement Scholarship Award gala. (USMC Official Photo)

With President Bill Clinton in the office of the secretary of defense for a reception following the signing the Defense Authorization Plan. (USMC Official Photo)

With William Cohen, former secretary of defense, at the Pentagon during the unveiling of the secretary of defense portrait, March 21, 2003. (USMC Official Photo)

Rita and I with comedian Drew Carey, a former Marine, at the Republican headquarters for the 2000 Presidential Inauguration. (Private Collection)

Speaking to a group of Marines in Afghanistan in December 2001. (USMC Official Photo)

President George W. Bush with First Lady Laura Bush, Rita, and me at the White House. (USMC Official Photo)

General James Jones with his wife, Diane, former secretary of state Henry Kissinger, Rita, and me. (USMC Official Photo)

With Senator John Warner at a Headquarters Marine Corps Congressional Breakfast on September 19, 2002. (USMC Official Photo)

With Bernard Shaw—a former Marine and former CNN anchor—and Rita. (Private Collection)

General Peter Pace, the general's wife, Lynn, Rita, and I. (Private Collection)

Rita and I with former president George H. W. Bush, who had been given the USO Patriot Award. (USMC Official Photo)

Signing the guest log at the New York Stock Exchange with Richard "Dick" Grasso, then chairman and chief executive of the NYSE. (Private Collection)

all of them to study hard, or mandated study groups. That seemed like the easiest path to failure.

Instead, I set up a system that ensured we were all prepared by making sure each Marine under me knew his material so well he could teach it to the rest of us.

"Joe, you are going to teach us all the physical security class tonight. We are all going to sit in class today and pay attention and gain as much knowledge as possible from the instructor. But tonight your job is to re-teach that class to the rest of us.

"Smith, you are going to reteach the classification class. Every one of us will expect you to know everything there is to know about that material. Tomorrow night, you are going to teach us that class."

Everybody had a class to reteach. I believe people need to own a part of whatever the group is trying to accomplish. Now that they had ownership, I upped the ante by creating competition within the group.

"Joe, don't let Smith do a better job teaching than you. You know what we need to know, so make sure you get us prepared. Don't let us know more than you."

Each person had been released, in effect, to focus on one aspect of the program. When it came time to take the tests, we had staff experts on every subject. They were able to compile lists of questions likely to appear on the tests. The process rocketed our scores. No detachment came close. My system made it easy for my people to produce. And if they knew how to produce, they would take pride of ownership in their subject. If they were proud, they would become inspired. If they were inspired, game over.

PLENTY OF TIME WAS sure spent working my way up to the executive wing in Washington, D.C., including a stop at the University of Minnesota from May 1983 to September 1985. I went there to prepare young men and women to become officers—leaders. I was young and not even a first sergeant when I arrived. A Navy chief was the senior enlisted person, and he reported to Captain Chauncey, the professor of naval science, who ran the program.

Years earlier I had learned every ribbon and exactly how and where it was to appear on a uniform. I knew no one really studied that kind of information, but to me it was all part of the package. I made myself an expert because I knew no one else would spend as much time as I did learning the information.

I also knew some Marines were not sure about whether to place a new ribbon they had been awarded above the Vietnam campaign ribbon, or below the NATO ribbon. All they knew is that they were required to wear them.

Was it a meaningless set of facts I had at my disposal? No, it was a difference maker. It was an edge. It was a small detail that allowed me to stay one step ahead. And all it took was preparation.

A case in point. Captain Chauncey had spent time in a POW camp in Vietnam; he had been shot down on Memorial Day in 1967.

One day, I saw that the captain's ribbons were out of sequence. I mentioned it to the chief, who didn't want to bother the captain with anything minor, particularly if it wasn't positive. I couldn't imagine having that kind of attitude. Here was a man who had served his country with dignity and heroism. I knew he didn't want to be walking around with those ribbons out of order.

"I'd like to speak to the captain."

"You're going to bother the captain with that?"

"Yes."

I went into the captain's office.

"Sir, I don't know if you realize it, but your ribbons are out of sequence."

"I've been wearing these ribbons this way since they were awarded and no one has ever said anything," he replied. "Thank you for taking the time to point it out."

He had taken dozens of official photographs with his ribbons out of place. So he was grateful that someone had the knowledge, interest, and fortitude to inform him of the discrepancy.

I ALWAYS FOUND MY inspiration from people of strong character around me, whether it was at home in Arkansas, on the drill field in San Diego, or at NATO headquarters in Brussels. The people who wore suits in Hot Springs were men who ran businesses and owned companies. They owned hotels, worked in management at the phone company, or operated the Reynolds Aluminum plant.

Another group of men wore coveralls and worked in the plants for those men. These were respectful men working at hotels, which was considered a very good job when I was growing up, or on the backs of garbage trucks. I respected those men, too, because they worked hard Monday through Friday, half a day on Saturday. They cleaned up Saturday afternoon and went to the grocery store with their wives. On Sunday, they went to church in a suit and tie with Stacy Adams shoes. Their cars were clean and well kept. These people didn't have much, but what they had they earned.

I respected the men in work clothes just as much as I respected the men in suits. What I realized, however, was that the men in the suits wrote the checks for the guys in the coveralls. So for me, now, I don't want my grandson, Andrew, growing up to be a star athlete such as Shaquille O'Neal. I want Andrew to be the man paying Shaquille O'Neal. The player has money. The owner has money and power.

I never had a problem with the idea of working my way up from the mailroom to the boardroom. Those men in the factory were dignified, hard working, and honest. They went to work with clean work clothes, a lunch pail filled with good food. They were a fine example, fuel for my desire to move my life forward. But I couldn't stop thinking about that other group. I remember dreaming about having a job that required me to wear a nice suit to my office in a tall building.

I eventually got that office in one of the largest buildings on earth, working in the Pentagon. And every day I walked into that office, I remembered those men in Hot Springs. Now that's the power of preparation.

6

Lead from the Heart:
Motivate by Compassion

MY GRANDMOTHER, IDA, WORKED on us from the head to the heart. It wasn't enough to know how to treat people. We needed to be compassionate. She wanted us to *feel* the difference between the right way and the wrong way. Then, in case we had any questions or doubts about the wisdom of her words, she backed them up with her own compassion.

The results? We were motivated to please her. The idea of failing to meet her expectations felt worse than anything my mother could dish out. My grandmother got the results she wanted without ever lifting a hand or raising her voice. It was a great lesson in leadership. I never forgot the wisdom in her approach even when it seemed irrelevant to the prevailing paradigm.

Nowhere is the idea of leading from the heart more at odds with the existing culture than on the drill field during boot camp. Everyone has seen the movie version of a Marine drill instructor or an Army drill sergeant screaming into the faces of young men and women frozen with fear. (Marines take pride in their attention to detail. We don't "drill" sergeants, so we don't have drill sergeants. We instruct drill.) There is a reason drill sergeants are portrayed that way in movies.

But there is a method to the madness. Drill is the number one factor when it comes to instilling discipline and order in a command. When you are on a battlefield, it's all about drill movements. We tell you to secure the right sector of the firing point. Those are commands that came from drilling. You can't function as a platoon, as a squad, or as a team in drill unless you are self-disciplined. Good order and discipline determine the welfare of that unit, and they come first from drill. And uniformity is what holds it all together.

In a similar way in business, cross-platform uniformity and consistency define many of the greatest and enduring global brands. Coca-Cola, McDonald's, Disney, Starbucks, and FedEx are some of the most successful and recognizable brands in the world. Whether you are in New York City; Tupelo, Mississippi; London; or Tokyo, quality and service standards are the same. Employees dress the same way, the stores and trucks are familiar. The experience is consistent.

In the military, we have complete control over our employees so we can establish and enforce our systems with something that approaches zero tolerance for deviation, because we constantly train our leaders and drill their subordinates to one day assume the roles of their bosses.

That's one reason I have never understand why drill instructors deal with mistakes by sending young recruits into a sand pit to improve performance. There are twenty to thirty drill marching movements and fifteen to twenty static (standing) movements. Each platoon is measured on every one of them. We have to make sure these movements are literally drilled into these recruits in basic training because it teaches them discipline and attention to detail. If they fail to pick up these movements and the ideas behind them, then they will be lost. If you have what we call a "rag-bag" platoon, then everyone associated with that platoon is judged accordingly.

If a recruit makes a mistake or fails to execute a marching movement exactly as it is taught, then an instructor will send the entire platoon into the sand pit to do jumping jacks or push-ups until sweat drips off of them like they have marched through the Mojave Desert. But when they finish, is the recruit—or the entire platoon for that matter—any more capable of executing the movement perfectly or eliminating whatever mistake that has precipitated the punishment?

From my perspective, the whole show represents an opportunity to make a difference. During every training cycle, four platoons compete to determine which one of them is the best. Those results are then measured against the results of every previous cycle. Records are kept, career paths determined. It's all about results.

So when I was a drill instructor and I saw another drill instructor leading his platoon into the sand, I'd take my recruits aside, put them into a half circle—what we call a "school circle"—and demonstrate once more exactly what I wanted. I used that opportunity not only to demonstrate but to motivate.

"See those men over there? They are getting sent to the pit because they made a mistake. They are going to finish those exercises. Their drill instructor is going to put them back on the parade deck just like you, but they are not going to be any smarter or any better than they were before they went into that pit. I believe in you. I believe you are better than that. So I have to teach you better. What I want you to do is pay attention and concentrate on what I am asking of you so we don't waste time over there in that pit doing something that doesn't even enhance your ability to perform. And when you compete against that platoon, you'll be competing with intelligence and understanding while they will be relying on muscle and fear. They will be tense, afraid of failing, because they have been taught that failure means a tour of that sand pit."

So now my platoon saw the process differently. They saw me taking care of them. All I did was create an atmosphere to instill in them the will to want to be better, to be the best. I knew that if I could get to their heart, I could make them want it. Then I didn't have to manipulate them into performing by using fear or other quick-fix methods. I got the discipline in. I made sure they saw my junior drill instructor as the guy who made their lives miserable. But they saw me as the leader who took care of them, the person who expected them to be better than all the other platoons.

I would put them into the pit when it was necessary, but not when it was unnecessary. If there was an opportunity to reiterate a point by teaching, then I preferred to teach those recruits how to do the moves correctly, rather than just put them in the sand until they got it. There were other ways to make up the discipline.

I wanted to inspire my privates to execute those drill movements the right way because they were going to drill them for the rest of their military career. It wasn't just about winning the drill competition. Everywhere they went, they would be expected to know how to march and execute those movements. So when I needed them to be focused on learning, I had their undivided attention. I didn't have their focus strained by the sand and sweat falling off their faces.

My platoons set records for initial drill and final drill competitions, some of which stood for years. You win those competitions and set those records not because you have especially good people and not because you are an especially good drill instructor. You win and set records by inspiring and motivating people to buy into the systems and ideas you put in place to make them successful.

The reality is that my report card was a reflection of how my platoon performed. The Marine Corps doesn't fire a recruit because he or she can't drill. They don't fire a drill instructor, either, but the road ahead doesn't become any easier for the leader of that failed recruit.

I APPLIED THE SAME principle years later when I was the Sergeant Major of Officer Candidate School (OCS) from 1991 to 1994. These were young candidates who were trying to become second lieutenants. Rather than lead by rank with two hands on the "book," I'd walk into their squad bay unannounced.

"What are you doing, Candidate?"

"I'm ironing this uniform for inspection, sir."

"There isn't a captain anywhere in the Marine Corps who can find fault with the way I iron a uniform. Let me show you how it's done."

Time to teach. Time to capture their will. To the rest of that squad bay it appeared as though I was only talking to Candidate Johnson, but I knew what the rest of them were doing. I talked loud enough so that all of them could hear. They were watching me and listening to every word. They wanted that edge.

"You take this leg and put it on the board," I said. "Start from the hem of the trousers at the bottom and you iron your way up. You follow the seams; lay it out and smooth it out."

They were amazed because I knew exactly how to make that leg look perfect. And I knew what they were thinking then, too.

"What a great sergeant major. He actually came in here to help us get through our inspection."

What they didn't know was that the first guy was in big trouble. The rest of them would be fine, but the guy whose trouser leg I had pressed now had to get the other leg to match and he didn't have a clue. And even if he did have a clue, he didn't have the experience. I knew all the tricks of the trade.

Then I'd walk over to another candidate who was shining his boot for inspection.

"There isn't a cow that ever lived that produced leather I couldn't shine. Let me show you how to do that."

I went through the entire process. I'm shining and I'm talking to him. Once again, all of them are listening and watching.

"You've got to use a circular motion. It's got to be from the heart. You have to feel it. Your fingers have to feel it. You have to talk to that leather so it can talk back with a shine. It's got to glow. It's got to make people recognize that when you put your foot into that boot, that boot is deserving of having a foot like yours."

Now that candidate is getting all pumped up because here is a superior showing him how to do something rather than screaming at him about something he didn't know how to do in the first place. But he was in as much trouble as the guy with the trousers. He had no chance of shining that other boot as well as I shined the first one. But I had made my point. They had heard me tell them what I expected, but now I had showed them, too. And I did it with respect. I had them.

I've always believed in the idea that who we really are shows most when no one is looking. How do you perform or go about your business when there's no one there to evaluate the effort, or grade the performance?

I never lost sight of that idea.

When I was sergeant major of OCS I had an instructor named Robinson come into my office one day looking for a fight. It was a reasonable expectation given the circumstances and the Marine culture. We were at Quantico, the Marine headquarters in northern Virginia, and the summer heat had settled into the otherwise pleasant surroundings.

I've spent a lot of time at Quantico over the years, starting with Embassy School training in 1979, and later from May 1991 to June

1994 as sergeant major of OCS. Quanitco is considered the cross-roads for the Marine Corps. Every officer trains there, and the enlisted usually find their way through there as well. The base itself, about twenty-five miles south of Washington, D.C., is bordered on one side by the Potomac River and covered with trees. The main road onto the base can be confusing for civilians because it takes them through rolling terrain with a tree-lined golf course on one side and houses on the other. It also has "Q Town," an old-fashioned downtown with shops, restaurants, bars, banks, and a Marine uniform store that serves the military and civilian populations.

Anyway, there are two increments of OCS every summer at Quantico, each one running roughly six weeks. These are grueling weeks with long hours and relentless stress for everyone involved. The course is designed to push candidates beyond their limits. It is nearly impossible to accomplish everything set out each day by intent. But the mental and physical demands are not limited to the candidates.

Every year I needed 103 platoon sergeants or enlisted men and women with drill instructor experience for the two increments. To say the least, it was a hard sell.

We rarely saw our families during the sessions; the days started at four in the morning and often didn't end until nine or ten at night—if one was lucky. The physical demands, which were extreme, were compounded by constant pressure to perform. Candidates had to deal with multiple demands, each of them depleting in its own way, while instructors not only had to put in the hours and participate in the physical training, but were responsible for making sure the candidates under them succeeded.

Virtually every person qualified to be an instructor did his or her best to avoid Quantico in the summer. A lot of these Marines had just been on the drill field at Parris Island, South Carolina, or in San Diego, or they had been to OCS in Quantico the summer before. I would spend the better part of the year trying to entice instructors to come teach OCS in Quantico by changing the prevailing mind-set. I let them know that OCS with me would be just as hard, but they would be treated with dignity and respect. They weren't going to be just fed to the process and put through the mill. I needed them—and I wanted them to know I understood that. Still, I heard every excuse imaginable and some that would have embarrassed small children.

"My toe hurts."

"My goldfish died."

You name it, I heard it.

Eventually, the Marine Corps threatened to sanction anyone who was called and who didn't show up. If you didn't want to come, fine. The Marine Corps would suspend your drill instructor certification. No Marine wanted that.

I had to find a way around the system, because I knew I couldn't change the system outright. So I sold the program all over the Marine Corps, all year long. Those who were ready for the first increment, I got them on board. Those who needed a little more time to develop or whose schedules required accommodation, I put in the second increment. They came in screaming and fighting because they didn't want to be there. Eventually, they left screaming and fighting because they didn't want to leave. This could never have been done without the support of Colonel Osmon. He understood the value of building families at OCS and he trusted me to do it with the instructors.

So one day a platoon sergeant named Robinson marched into my office. She had petitioned the Marine Corps for a three-week delay in her assignment to Quantico that had been denied. I'm not sure whether anyone took the time to find out why she needed the extra time. Either way, she had been shipped off to Quantico as scheduled. It took courage to come to me the way she did. I knew that. I also knew that kind of courage, particularly in a situation where rank trumps all, is the kind born of anger and frustration.

That step into my office would have been the last step she took as a Marine with a lot of other sergeants major. If she lasted long enough to make her point, it would have been met with a lecture about loyalty to the institution. She would have been reminded of what it meant to be a Marine, with words such as dedication, commitment, and responsibility. Of course, when the speech ended she wouldn't have any of those feelings for the Marine Corps, and the Corps wouldn't have any idea why she'd stormed into the room in the first place.

Now other people in my position may have understood and appreciated her dilemma. But for me, what needed to be done was self-evident.

Turns out, besides being a Marine, Robinson was a mother. And her only daughter was going to graduate from a high school in California in less than a week. But this Marine was now stuck 3,000 miles away.

"You people," she said. "You people are going to make me miss the graduation of my only child. I told everyone I needed only a three-week delay. No one listened."

As the sergeant major of OCS, I knew I needed her committed to what we were trying to get done. I had to have her mind, not just her body. So I listened. By that point in my career, I understood that listening better up front usually meant having to do less on the back end. Besides, I knew this Marine because she had been a student when I was director of the Staff Noncommissioned Officer (NCO) Academy in El Toro, California. She had heard the speeches I gave every Friday about the importance of family and leadership at home as I recapped the week. I wanted my students to understand that even if it hadn't been an easy week, it hadn't been a dismal week, either.

"You have had a hard week with some successes and some fumbles. But don't carry the week home with you. Take a few minutes to appreciate that what your spouses have been doing is just as important as the hard work you put in here. They have been taking care of your children, cleaning the house, picking up groceries. Many of them are probably picking up that cold beer for you right now. Take your leadership home. Don't walk into the house so geared up by what you have been through at school that you don't appreciate the tribulations your spouse and children have had to deal with. Your children have had to sleep in a house without you home all week.

"If you go home and stir up a hornet's nest and come back here upset, then you have to deal with me and instructors who will bring you back to reality in a hurry. Don't be ashamed to tell your wife or husband you love them. Allow them to help you get ready to come back here Monday with a positive attitude so you can be successful in the week ahead of you."

I always talked about the love Marines had for their families. The younger ones, usually gung-ho young men and women who had committed themselves to the Marine Corps, did so around the same time they had committed to marriage. I didn't want them running up the mountain on the way to being a great Marine and finding out their foundation was made of sand. It's easy to forget about home life when the business of the Marine Corps is so consuming. A lack of balance and compassion for the other person can lead to tension and very quickly can turn into anger.

I'm sure a measure of Robinson's courage came from the possibility, however small, that I might actually practice what I preach.

"I'm leaving to see my only daughter graduate," she said in a huff. "I know you are going to punish me, so go ahead and do whatever you have to do. But I am leaving."

"I am only going to punish you if you don't already have a plane ticket," I said. "You need to see your daughter graduate. She will only graduate from high school once. You'll have plenty of opportunities to train candidates."

It was hard to tell if the look on her face showed more relief or surprise.

"You mean, you're not going to chew me out about Marine Corps loyalty?" she asked. "And lecture me about what true Marines do?"

I explained that I was doing exactly what Marines do. Marines take care of one another. I needed to take care of her, so she could take care of her family. And if she took care of her family, she'd be ready to come back and take care of the Marine Corps.

To me that's a universal concept not unique to the military. I don't care if you are running a business or coaching a professional sports team, treating people with dignity and respect is the only way to inspire and build commitment.

According to policy, we both knew she never should have come directly to me, of course. That wasn't the proper chain of command. But somehow she found the strength to approach me, flex her muscles, and speak her mind. For all she knew, she risked getting bounced out of my office, and the Marines.

She left feeling lighter, but confused. She came expecting a fight over something there was no need to fight about.

What is the lesson in leadership?

Simple. Not everyone coming through the door is the same. You need to treat each and every person as an individual of importance. I never allowed myself to take her actions personally. She came to me because she knew I could help her, but she didn't know how to articulate her needs. If I had chosen not to listen to her because she hadn't approached me through the proper channels, what would have been accomplished? I wouldn't have known why she was there and I certainly wouldn't have understood her problem. Nothing positive would have transpired in those moments or in the weeks and months ahead.

I needed to take the time to listen so I could understand what the conversation was really about. If a person in charge feels it necessary to cite the organization's pecking order rather than listen, then he isn't confident enough in his ability to fix the situation in the first place.

She returned more dedicated, more responsible, and a better Marine. Why? The Marines had treated her with respect by using common sense rather than delivering a lecture from an operator's manual.

Would she have been as good and loyal and committed a Marine if her request had been arbitrarily refused? If she'd been turned away and allowed to stew in resentment toward the military and guilt about her daughter, what kind of Marine would I have?

I knew the answer intuitively.

Integrating compassion into leadership made sense not only because it was the right thing to do. It also helped me produce results. I always wanted to leave whatever unit I led, or whatever job I had, better than it was before I arrived. That meant paying attention to issues and spending time with people regardless of what the book said.

My concern for those Marines under me never stopped at the office. It extended into their private lives as well.

When I was in Puerto Rico from 1986 to 1988, I had young, entry-level Marines who were at their first duty station. They would see these beautiful girls, and because Puerto Rico is a commonwealth unlike the Philippines, for example, there is nothing to keep them from getting married. I never talked anyone out of getting married. In fact, I encouraged them to get married. But I also showed them that marriage had to be done at the right time, with the right person, when the right resources were in place—in that order. I knew my people, so I knew when one of them had fallen for a local girl and was contemplating marriage, however preposterous the idea might be under the circumstances.

"So you met a girl?"

"Yes, sir."

"Is she beautiful?"

"Yes, she is, sir."

"She probably had her makeup on, her hair was done real nice, and she was wearing her best clothes when you two met."

"Yes, sir."

"Do you know how much makeup costs? Do you know how much it costs for a woman to have her hair done? Do you know what women's clothes cost? Tell you what. I'll get you a piece of paper and you write down what those things cost so we can talk about what it takes to support a wife."

Of course, he had no idea what a bottle of nail polish cost.

"See, son, the problem is you have to provide all those things when you get married. Her father doesn't do that any longer. That's your responsibility. If you can't supply those things, then friction that neither one of you will see coming can infect your relationship. You may think the only issues that cause friction in a marriage are whether you remain faithful, or whether or not you are abusive in any way. That's not true. There are other demands such as providing financial security, meeting her emotional needs and those of your children. They can produce pain if you are not prepared. You have to secure your ability to manage those issues before you bring others into your life. All that disposal cash you think you have right now gets disposed of very quickly with a wife, a house, and a car. But let me know when you are getting married. I'd love to attend."

Now, I didn't just talk to one of them. When I talked to these Marines about marriage, I always asked the young man to bring his fiancée into my office.

"Where are the two of you going to live?"

"With my parents," she might say.

"Do you know military rules on marriage and living outside the base? It's simple. If we bring a Marine to Puerto Rico unaccompanied and he gets married, then he's still unaccompanied until he applies for a change in status. He can't get married and move into a house down the street. And do you know how long that takes?"

I walked them through the application and all the minefields that he didn't have time to consider because he was too busy being in love, even though he'd only been there a month.

"And, oh by the way, he's not going to be here very long. He's got exactly twenty-two months left, then he's going to rotate to another duty station. He might be in North Carolina. He could go to California. Wherever he goes it's probably only going to be for three weeks to two months, then he'll be on a ship for six months. Now, your English isn't very good and you don't have a feel for the American culture, so there's a good chance you will be miserable in a foreign place by yourself. But you can do it because you love one another. I know you can do it."

Most of them never did it. But I never told them not to get married. I just wanted them to understand what marriage really meant, particularly in the military. What I loved about those days was the idea I could affect the lives of these young people by educating them on issues no one had ever talked to them about before.

Other times, an opportunity to provide insight and education arose amid conflict. I had a Marine in Okinawa, Japan, sent to me on his way to being court-marshaled. I had just taken over the 1st Marine Aircraft Wing (MAW) in November 1995, which meant I was in charge of all aviation in the Pacific between Hawaii and Japan. No enlisted Marines saw the general without going through me and that's where that young man was headed.

He had crossed two bridges on a road that led out of the Marine Corps. There is zero tolerance for the use of racial slurs. Combined with physical assault his punishment would be severe. Either he would be court-marshaled, which would create a permanent stain on his record for life, or he could receive Nonjudicial punishment (NJP), which meant he accepted whatever came next and moved on.

We've all heard the phrase, "pick your poison." Sometimes taking NJP makes even a court-marshal sound preferable. This Marine could have ended up in the brig, had his pay and rank reduced, or paid a fine among other things.

Now this could have been very easy, given my position and the fact we were Marines. I could have spent five minutes lecturing him about his behavior, alerted the general, and moved on. Instead I decided to listen. Later on he told me we spent eight hours in that office. He was close. It was actually eight hours and twenty minutes. In that time, I had an opportunity to tighten up that loose screw, rather than send him down the road on a wobbly wheel with no knowledge of how to fix that car. I didn't want to see that kid continue to be a danger to himself and others.

Here's the point. It was a serious issue. But it wasn't so bad that I couldn't work with him and help him understand how to change his behavior and attitude.

I could have taken the traditional sergeant major route and told him, "The General said we are punishing you this way, and you are out of here."

But it was important for me to look deeper into this kid's heart. He had to understand what he did wrong and how his actions had affected other people. And the fact is, while completely out of line, his interpretation of the events wasn't 100 percent wrong. Part of the problem was the Marine culture. If I tell you to do something, damn it, then do it, and don't ask me why, how, or when. Just do it the way I say and how I say it.

I couldn't explain the crippling effect of his actions in a five-minute lecture. He was a seasoned Marine, but I tried to deal with young kids straight out of basic training the same way. They would get punished. But I never abandoned them. I never accepted the possibility that just because a Marine was punished, that meant he was now a bad apple for the rest of his military career. I saw an opportunity when that happened. I saw the chance to rehabilitate that person into a better Marine, better than he might have been had he not been punished. We put too much into these Marines to dismiss them when they make a mistake, even when it's a serious one.

The military often doesn't take the time to look inside that soldier to see how we might fix that one leak so we can retain the entire bucket. Instead, all we see is the leak. We tell everybody the bucket is broken and throw it away. Then we come get your son or daughter to fill that space. To many, these Marines are like bolts on a Humvee. Leaders need to recognize the fact one flaw isn't necessarily evidence of complete and irreversible incompetence.

My Marine wasn't about to get a pass. What he got was a mind shaping. We didn't talk about the punishment because that was up to the general. The outcome was going to be the same whether we talked five minutes or five days. But I wanted him to understand why he was guilty. He needed to know that he had to change his behavior before his career was damaged beyond repair.

I didn't believe in saying we took care of our people only as long as they fit into the mold we created for them. It comes back to a very fundamental question about values.

What do you do when the book says you don't have to do anything?

You do the right thing and lead from the heart.

7

Rebuild What You Tear Down: Nurture Self-Esteem

FAT BODIES."

That's what most of the young men standing before me were called. In the unique lexicon of the United States Marine Corps, that label is stamped onto recruits who arrive out of shape. Some of them make it into a regular platoon as scheduled, then wash out into the physical conditioning platoon (PCP) because they aren't strong enough or fit enough to compete. Being sent off to PCP is not an encouraging beginning to the challenging, if not menacing, twelve-week process of reconstruction that is Marine boot camp.

I had just been through my own test six months earlier at Drill Instructor School (DI School), one of the most intense training programs in the Marine Corps. The qualifications are designed to separate the good from the potentially great. A Marine must be at least twenty-one years old due to the mental, physical, and emotional demands of the course. Every record is checked, every score evaluated. Even your finances are reviewed. If you can't take care of yourself, then you aren't capable of taking care of new recruits.

Once I passed the screening process, orders were cut and I was sent to DI School in San Diego, which seemed fitting. I was barely three years removed from my own boot camp experience. The physical demands of DI School are complicated by the fact that you are not only executing every element of the training regimen, but you are learning how to teach the process at the same time.

Recruits learn to march in formation, which is a challenge for all of them at the beginning. At DI School we learn how to teach those movements. It isn't enough to know them. We have to be able to recite each of the many movements verbatim with not a single word out of order. Everything about the process is detail oriented to the extreme, with the expectation of perfection. Plenty of people never make it out of DI School.

What makes the process so challenging is that students are held to exacting standards every minute of every day. We were checked constantly and randomly. For example, I could be sitting in class and the instructor suddenly announces a locker inspection. Or maybe he says we have to go back to our room and change into another uniform. If you got up late and you didn't have your locker squared away, or if your other uniform isn't perfect, then DI School might not be for you.

As a result, Marine Corps drill instructors are about as close to perfection as people come. Everything about them is perfect. Their uniforms are immaculate at all times, they are groomed to the letter of the code, they are as physically fit as anyone anywhere in the military and all of them speak with authority and confidence without even the slightest hint of self-doubt. The only Marines more "squared away," if that's possible, are DI School instructors, the professors of perfection.

I graduated from Drill Instructor School February 22, 1974, two days before my twenty-second birthday, at 10:00 A.M. By 3:00 P.M. I was working. As one of two junior drill instructors reporting to a senior drill instructor, I started with a brand-new platoon right off the bus. And I stayed with those recruits every day and most nights.

There are only males at basic training in San Diego. Men and women train at Parris Island, South Carolina. At that time, the normal work cycle for a junior instructor was to work one day, then have a day or a day and a half off. There were no days off for me. From the time those recruits woke up to reveille to the time they went to bed and until a couple of hours after they went to sleep, I worked to learn everything there was to know. I didn't care how much experience the senior drill instructors had, I wanted to know at least as much as fast as possible. Some of them had families, which meant outside obligations that distracted their focus. I was young and hungry.

Sometimes, one of the older junior drill instructors wanted to take off early even when he was on duty.

"Are you going to be here, McMichael? I've got some things to do. You don't mind sleeping with the dinks, do you?"

"Not at all. See you in the morning."

Among the many derogatory names, new recruits are called "dinks." Staying with them, however, was never a problem for me because a lot of things go on at night. My knowledge gap closed very quickly. I created an edge. Halfway through training my first platoon, I had learned what normally takes at least two full platoon cycles.

The physical fitness and teaching aspects are elements I naturally enjoy. But I realized early on that leadership is a craft, almost an art form that had to be learned. I had seen the old-fashioned screamer depicted in movies, and I had experienced superiors with a more refined touch who seemed to produce better results. I wanted to understand the mechanics and nuances required to motivate people. I had the power to demand performance and I had all the time-proven tools at my disposal. I could threaten, scream in their faces, and punish them into performing.

But I couldn't get out of my head the fact I had been in their shoes. I had been commanded to do things that were neither the right way nor the best way. But as a subordinate, you do what you are told, no questions asked. There is no other way to get through the Marine Corps training regimen.

When the roles were reversed, I found I had no desire to inflict the kind of pain that had been once inflicted on me. Every aspect of training in the Marine Corps is geared to produce results. Recognition of that fact and a desire to be the best allowed me to ascend very quickly. Leaders are identified, challenged, and tested every day in the Marine Corps. Drill instructors are no different. They compete against all the other drill instructors to be named best platoon in each twelve-week cycle. Records are kept, winners are acknowledged, and careers fast-tracked or slowed to a crawl as a result. The way to create distance between your platoon and another seemed clear to me. Produce better results faster and more efficiently.

I look at it this way. Coca-Cola could have produced what we now call Classic Coke forever. Or the company could create a new product like Diet Coke to compete more effectively and maintain market share.

In a highly structured, precedent-laden institution like the Marine Corps, the kind of change I instituted was as foreign as a foreign language. Maintaining the status quo means making those young men as miserable, confused, and unhappy as possible. I understand the value of the teardown process.

But rebuilding is at least as important. Eventually one leads to the other, but I couldn't understand the logic supporting the existing paradigm.

The point of basic training is to train recruits to become real Marines. In the old days, they learned by being busted upside the head, kicked in the butt, and dragged around by the nose. That approach guarantees recruits to jump when they are asked to jump. The only problem is the recruit had no idea why he was being asked to jump. As a matter of fact, he didn't even know how high he was supposed to jump.

I wanted to work with their minds as well as their bodies to create a better Marine. I knew I wasn't the only person who could come up with answers. So I created systems that would allow for the input of these others within the parameters I established.

That's how I have set up every unit or organization I have ever led. And it all started by focusing on results rather than the "show."

There's no question my approach went against the grain, but I didn't want a litter of Pavlov's dogs. I wanted Marines who understood what we were doing, why we were doing it, and how to do it the absolute best way.

For example, we marched on black asphalt in San Diego. After the first day, you saw recruits with beet red skin. Their ears, noses, and necks were sunburned. The second day they were blistered, and by the third day they were miserable. My recruits didn't have any blisters. They weren't red, either.

"What's the smell?" other drill instructors would ask.

"Sunscreen."

It made perfect sense to me. While they were telling recruits, "It's the Lord's sun. Let it burn you," I wanted to keep my recruits safe and in the fight. The other instructors were playing silly games with their recruits whose ears were bleeding, while mine were going about their business focused on their roles. Call the other instructors Hollywood if you like, but I was taking care of somebody else's children while they were allowing their recruits' skin to burn.

Midway through my second cycle, I was made senior drill instructor and given my own platoon.

Recruits are picked up at the airport and taken to the San Diego recruit depot. From the minute they arrive at the depot, someone is screaming at them.

"Where are your bags, recruit?"

"Did you forget your bags?"

"Refer to me as 'sir.' Is that clear?"

"Now where are those bags?"

It doesn't matter where you come from or what you have experienced, the process is disorientating. These kids have no idea what's happening. Most of them are scared to death. I can't think of what might prepare a young man for the ground shaking that comes with boot camp.

Once there are enough recruits to create a series—four platoons—then another twelve-week cycle begins. The Fat Bodies are worked hard so they can be moved out of PCP and into a regular platoon. Still, they are perceived as the worst of the worst.

The new recruits are in shock. They are being screamed at virtually every minute in a place that looks like no place they have ever seen. They are being run around like a bunch of wild cattle out on the range with no idea about what's happening. It's a nightmare for these boys. They are rushed into the barbershop to have their heads shaved. We run them through a shower like a bunch of prisoners. From a drill instructor's perspective, the idea is to put the fear of God into them immediately so positions are established quickly and clearly. You represent their only hope. They are uncomfortable and scared with absolutely no idea of what is about to hit them.

My platoon consisted of a combination of Fat Bodies and new recruits. No one knew the difference, and I didn't tell them. The imbalance could have made the process more difficult, but I short-circuited that by putting the Fat Bodies in charge. There are four squads in a platoon, and Fat Bodies became the squad leaders. It's a coveted honor to carry the flag for the platoon. One of the Fat Bodies got that job, too, because he had seen what the process looked like.

Mentally, many of my recruits were four chapters into the story before the new guys even got the book. The new recruits were puzzled and scared, but they gravitated toward the Fat Bodies. They were just thankful somebody was there who could help keep me off their butts.

It didn't take me long to realize our strength was exactly what every other drill instructor saw as our weakness. Victory had been served up to me on a silver platter. My recruits had already been around the base for three to five weeks. They understood a lot more than the new recruits coming in off the bus. They had been screamed at and they had seen the entire process unfold all around them. They knew where the medical and dining facilities were. They had drilled in a military installation for weeks. The new recruits couldn't even open the combination lock on their C-bags, which held all their gear. They were so discombobulated by the intensity and speed of change, that they had to write their locker combinations on their bodies. They couldn't remember three numbers.

Marching is a big deal in boot camp, and it's not nearly as easy as it appears. Every movement has to be learned and perfected to be in sync with the group. The first few days are chaos. My recruits watched other platoons walking down the street holding hands, locked arm and arm, trying to learn how to march. The majority of my platoon already knew how to march. I had to correct some of the Fat Bodies, but refining their movements allowed the others to learn faster. And I talked to them constantly about what they could accomplish, how they were actually the best platoon on the grounds. Instead of focusing on their weaknesses, I nurtured their strengths.

While the other platoons were so confused they couldn't figure out where to eat, my recruits fell into formation and headed straight to chow. I'd give a command, and they would start marching. It looked like a parade. I could see the other platoons watching us. I could even see the other drill instructors watching my recruits. We were in their heads the first week and we never got out.

Those other platoons couldn't imagine being as good as we were because of how far ahead we were from opening day. I wanted them to fear us for no real reason other than the fact they had no idea how we were able to learn so quickly. They didn't know our platoon was the fat group with weeks of experience. Their drill instructors knew, but they didn't see the opportunity. Those recruits had to be wondering why their drill instructors hadn't taught them what my recruits knew. And indirectly, I'd remind my recruits of that, too.

"I taught you these movements today because of how smart you are. You must be smart because you are learning quickly. So when you see those other platoons, notice how far ahead you are, how fast you are improving."

By the time the other platoons realized my recruits were the rejects and not the shining examples they appeared to be, it was too late. We were too far ahead.

Our advantage was seniority. Our disadvantage was obvious. We probably weren't going to win the fitness competition, but we could win the other ten events. We could be the best marksmen and we could know the practical application material better than anyone else. Recruits had to learn every rank and be able to identify by chevron the difference between them. The test was verbal, no pencil and paper, no wrong answers. They had to be perfect.

"What is in the middle of a master gunnery sergeant's chevron?"

"Bursting bomb, sir."

"What's the difference between the chevrons on a first sergeant and a master sergeant?"

"A first sergeant has a diamond in the middle of his chevron, sir. A master sergeant has crossed rifles, sir."

At night, I talked to them about how they could get their hearts and minds into the process so they could be better than the platoon next door. If I gave them a command, they wanted to do it right. I was hard on them, but I didn't humiliate them or make their lives miserable for sport. I instilled a desire to excel in my recruits while the other drill instructors were trying to manipulate performance with threats.

The weakest point in any organization is usually its mental approach. Mental toughness can overcome physical limitations just as discipline can triumph over talent. My recruits might not have won a hand-to-hand fight, but their experience made them mentally superior.

There are three phases to boot camp and all of them are evaluated. After the first two weeks, platoons are graded on basic drill movements, for example. Every drill instructor wants to win what is called "initial drill" because it can set the tone for the rest of the cycle. That's exactly what happened. We won initial drill and rode that wave of energy all the way to the end.

"Final drill" is the payoff. That's where the winners shine and everyone knows exactly who they are. The reviewing stands are full of drill instructors and officers from around the base. For the platoons, including the drill instructors, it's the Super Bowl.

My recruits were so impressive they won convincingly by the time they reached graduation day.

Some of these recruits had changed so much they were unrecognizable. I had one young man who lost thirty-five pounds. His parents walked right by him. He wasn't the same fat kid with the soft body who left home a few months earlier. Now he looked like a physically fit, handsome young Marine.

The Fat Bodies no longer existed in mind or spirit. In fact, the entire process made them better because they had not only transformed themselves physically, but they had gone from the worst to the best in twelve weeks. There wasn't anything those recruits didn't think they could accomplish after that.

THE MARINES I HAD in Puerto Rico were straight out of entry level training. Most of them had never been out of their home state until boot camp, and now they were off the mainland with a modicum of freedom. I had the privilege of working there as first sergeant for Major Butch Morgan, a great leader and a better man. Butch reinforced the idea that leaders don't give up on people, particularly young people.

When these young men and women would make mistakes, it was customary for the punishment to often continue in one form or another long after it officially ended. These Marines were labeled as bad apples, and their careers suffered as a result.

I couldn't accept that. We invested too much in these Marines to dismiss them when they made a mistake. Instead of trying to fix that one leak, even if it took many tries, the entire bucket was tossed aside.

"That one's no good. Let's get somebody else's son or daughter."

Whether in business or the military, the money and effort expended to recruit, train, and establish someone on the job is significant. Why not take five minutes to see if you can touch that person in a way that motivates them?

I developed certain systems that came close to eliminating most of my Marines' mistakes. But I had to be present in person or spirit at all times. I had to be engaged in their lives beyond the Marines Corps. I needed to know what was happening at all times, the quality of the atmosphere, the tempo of the unit. If something went wrong, I wanted it to be a crack not an explosion. I could apply glue to a crack. An explosion didn't leave many options.

As Major Morgan's first sergeant, we worked together to run the day-to-day operations. He was one of the greatest leaders I worked for in the Marine Corps. Butch never backed down from a problem, and he never failed to stand up for what was right regardless of the politics involved. In that sense, we shared common ground. He was tough but he was fair.

If we were doing our jobs, then we handed out the right amount of punishment for any mistake. But we also worked to bring that Marine back into the unit so he could reclaim his reputation. Part of that approach was to explain the punishment up front. I would talk to a young Marine about what happened and try to prepare him to recover. The Marine would be punished. No value would come from eliminating the consequences of negative behavior, even if it were possible.

But once the punishment was done, I would invite him to play basketball with the leadership that day at lunch. I might go out of my way to say hello, or stop and talk to the young man. I wanted him to know he wasn't blacklisted. He needed to understand leaders took care of a good Marine even when he missed the mark.

Major Morgan and I worked to rebuild these Marines' credibility by restoring their confidence. I might put that Marine out front during the run that day. Or I'd help that person work to be named Marine of the Month, which is a big deal. I never wanted to put a shelf life on people. They were still somebody's sons. If everyone was perfect, then why would anyone need a first sergeant or a commanding officer?

WHEN I WAS THE DET commander at the U.S. embassy in Denmark in 1979, I made a point never to read what we called the "counseling sheet" that came in a sealed folder with any new Marine assigned to the unit. It held a detailed evaluation of that Marine by his old commander. The minute a Marine handed his sheet to me, I turned around and threw it into the garbage unopened.

That could be dangerous gesture, but I was willing to take the risk. The Marine had no idea what had just happened.

"I'm not interested in your counseling sheet. I am only interested in what you do from this moment forward. If you come in here with a perfect score of 300 points in the physical fitness test, what good does that do me now? I can't use an old performance today.

"If you have come with a hiccup in your old embassy duty, I assume you have seen the light and are now committed to being the best Marine you can become. You have that chance. Now you know you are not going to be judged based on whatever mistakes you made before. Nor are you going to be judged by whatever wonderful things you did in the past. You will be judged solely by what you do here and now. I don't care what your old boss had to say about you. I will look at what you are supposed to do at this embassy and judge you on that performance."

If that Marine had messed up previously, then he no longer had to walk around with a cloud over his head. It was a fresh start. If he was a perfect Marine, then he didn't get to walk around feeling superior. He had to prove himself to me.

Look at great athletes. Most of them are paid on the basis of past performance. A baseball owner pays Alex Rodriguez millions of dollars because he is betting the player's future performance will match his past.

I put everybody on a one-year, make-good contract.

General Jones has always said no one wakes up in the morning committed to making a mistake that could end his or her military career. People make mistakes. Good leaders have to determine whether it's an honest mistake, or one done with malice. Good owners have to know whether a player's effort will be softened or further hardened by a massive pay raise.

I CONTINUED WITH THE same approach once I was Sergeant Major of the Marine Corps working out of the Pentagon. When somebody found trouble, I'd look for something positive that person was doing and send over a note. If we were out in public, I'd call out that person so everyone knew the sergeant major still believed in him. It was important that that Marine understood, even after a mistake, however large or small, that the entire Corps hadn't turned against him.

"Hey, if the sergeant major thinks I'm okay, then I must be all right."

I needed him to feel comfortable coming back into the fold.

It was no different than when I was in high school and a young lady, a friend of mine, came back to school after having a baby. That was back in the mid to late 1960s when having a child out of wedlock, much less in high school, left a mark that never went away. If we were friends before the baby, then why would that change now that she had a family? In my mind, she needed friends more than ever at that point.

That lesson was part of my childhood education. It didn't come from the Marine Corps. I learned the value of people at the dinner table. I saw how to value people by the way my mother and grandmother treated everyone. If one of us got in trouble at home, the other siblings would form a little cocoon. We didn't abandon one another if somebody just got a spanking. We wanted to help them recover so we could all go back out and play.

"Always love your sisters and brothers," my grandmother would say. "Take that same affection and commitment to the community. There's something good in everybody. All you have to do is look."

I HAVE APPLIED THAT principle to Marines at every leadership position I've held even though it often wasn't consistent with the prevailing culture.

Officer Candidate School (OCS) is a good example of an environment designed to screen and evaluate. The men and women assigned to OCS are supposed to be the elite. The instructors are, in theory at least, one step ahead. But not all of them arrive in perfect condition for one reason or another. As sergeant major of OCS in Quantico, Virginia, I had a choice. I could eliminate people during their screening or I could invest time in their development.

I had a young lady who arrived six months after giving birth to her first child. Her maternity time had expired and she was scheduled to be an instructor at OCS. Clearly her body wasn't back into Marine condition. She hadn't lost all her excess weight and her fitness level wasn't consistent with Marine Corps standards, much less the demands of the job. But I knew that instructors came from all walks of life, every occupation in the military. I couldn't define them as Marines without also acknowledging their other roles in life. In this case, the Marine also was a wife and mother.

One day an officer criticized this young woman about her weight.

"She's not a good example of what a Marine is supposed to be. She's out of shape and overweight."

"That might be so," I told him. "But what you have failed to do is look around at the rest of your colleagues. Some of them are not in the best shape, either. If all you looked at was her weight and physical condition, then that's all you would see. But this is only day three of eight weeks. What you don't see is how all the other candidates gravitate toward her and how well she motivates them. Look a little closer and maybe you'll see something more than extra weight. And by the way, be thankful you will never be in the position of trying to reclaim your Marine body within six months of delivering a child, after nine months of carrying one."

Compassion and common sense are powerful tools. All it took was a little compassion to appreciate what that Marine had been through. I prided myself on using those tools even when it meant telling a superior something he didn't want to hear. Applying common sense and compassion was always the most practical way to derive optimum results with the least difficulty.

ATTITUDES FORMED BY RULES rather than common sense can result in failed leadership. At Marine Security Guard School, as at every stop up the command ladder, competition is layered throughout the entire process. Instructors compete to have the best detachment at the end of the class. Just like in boot camp, the competition between instructors is intense. In fact, most of the instructors at MSG have been drill instructors. At MSG, however, instructors have an extra arrow in their quivers. Students are evaluated three or four weeks into the program. Instructors can recommend the elimination of weak candidates. In fact, many of them think they have a vested interest in eliminating rather than working to strengthen the weak links. By tossing them out, instructors improve their chances of having the best detachment in the school.

What these "leaders" fail to recognize is that by losing a student they have failed at functional leadership. I know Joe might not get to the next level as quickly as John. What takes John two weeks to understand and execute might take Joe the entire training cycle. When I was there I never wanted to drop anyone too early in the training cycle.

First, I trusted myself enough to know I could reach even the weakest student. Second, I'm a very good judge of character, so I was willing to use the full eight weeks of instruction. Why not? If we were so smart that we could separate the good from the bad in just three weeks, then why not eliminate the other five weeks of training?

The first evaluation comes roughly midway through the program at MSG. I made sure I understood exactly where my students were not only in the program but with the rest of their lives. If something outside MSG was interfering with their performance, then I wanted to know so I could help them through that distraction. I reviewed where they were and how they stacked up. There might be a couple of late arrivals noted. Maybe some scores weren't as good in one or more skills as they should have been. Put those things together and a student might appear fragile or at serious risk.

I would talk to them about where they were relative to where they started. No one went backward, so I focused on their improvement rather than their deficiencies. I knew these Marines would be fine by the end of the school. All they needed was a strategy that helped secure the time they needed.

"If you think where you were when you started, then you look a lot stronger. More important, look at where you want to be in all these areas at the end of the eight weeks. Based on your improvement so far, you are going to get there. But that can't happen if you are flushed out of the process during evaluations. So here is how you are going to present your case. When you go before the board you are going to be asked, 'Do you think you should be here?'

"Tell them, 'I have failed some of the inspections, but I have completed 80 percent of them and I am working hard on the other 20 percent. I am confident I will pass all the necessary inspections and tests by the time these eight weeks are over.' You will have taken the steam out of their objections by eliminating the negative and accentuating the positive."

THE MARINE CORPS IS as demanding an environment as exists. But it is critical, particularly in an environment with such high expectations, that leaders provide a pat on the back with as much enthusiasm as when they slam poor performance and behavior. I always wanted my Marines to be aware of me watching them do well, so they would become more conscious of their actions when I wasn't around.

If they knew I appreciated their positive efforts then I didn't have to be by their side at all times. That's not to say I didn't point out their faults and demand greatness. They simply needed to know that I recognized small successes, effort, and commitment as well.

We are all valuable in someone's eyes. If I have $1 million in crisp $100 bills and offer to give them away with no strings attached, virtually everyone will take the money. Now, what if I crumple up every one of those $100 bills and throw them into a large trash container. Will the average person hesitate before jumping into that trash to find the money? I don't think so. What if I take that trash, throw it into the snow and mud? Will anyone think any differently about all those $100 bills? Not likely. It's still $1 million dollars, and no one will lose sight of that fact. In other words, it doesn't matter how dirty, smelly, or wet those dollars become. None of those flaws affect their value.

It's the same with people. No matter how many mistakes we make or how many disappointments we experience, we are no less valuable than the day we were born. Even though I worked inside an organization dedicated to perfection, I expected people to continue to realize and improve upon their value.

And I saw many of those same people rise above and go beyond what they expected of themselves. That's why I have dedicated myself to the development of future leaders since retiring from the Marine Corps in 2006.

At the request and on behalf of Joe Murphy, an extremely successful banker and former Marine in New York City, I work with young men at New York's Rice High School on the corner of 124th Street and Malcolm X Boulevard in Harlem. Rice, named after Edmund Rice, the founder of the Congregation of Christian Brothers, who run the school, is also is an acronym for Responsibility, Integrity, Courage, and Excellence.

It's not easy for parents to get their children into Rice, and it's not easy for those children once they are accepted. Boys wear white shirts and ties, a uniform that makes them different from every other kid in their neighborhood. The vast majority come from single-parent households where that parent works at least one job.

Discipline is at a premium and expectations are not modified no matter the personal circumstance. The results speak for themselves. In 2007, 100 percent of the senior class graduated, all of them were accepted at a college or university, and every one qualified for some form of financial aid. The students know why they are at Rice. My job is to make sure they don't lose hope in the face of challenges, personal and otherwise, between the first year and the last.

I asked a group of them to tell me what child support meant to them.

"It's the money my dad is supposed to give my mom every week."

"That's not child support. That is a monetary obligation placed on your father by a judge in a court of law. It's not child support. Child support by my definition is being a father who is there for soccer practice, who talks to you about how school went today, who puts you to bed at night, educates you about how to handle an allowance, and how you treat your sisters and brothers. That's child support."

One day I was told about a young man who had become disruptive. No one seemed to know whether he would make it or not, based on his recent behavior. So we sat down to talk. For some reason, I asked him the date of his birthday.

"Last weekend," he said.

I walked him backward through the week. It turns out his father had failed to show up as promised. And he still hadn't delivered the present he promised, either.

"So why am I going to school? Why am I trying to be a good kid? Why am I obeying all these rules? What difference does it make? The people who are supposed to love me don't care enough to show up on my birthday."

"The answer is that you need to love yourself independently of everyone else. You have to love yourself completely before you can ever love anyone else adequately. You have to be proud of what you do, and do it so well that people remember the positive mark you left. You can't do that if you don't love yourself."

This young boy was an only child. His mother worked, his father was absent. He was confused. Yet he told me that he was going to be "important."

"What is it that you want to do with your life?"

"I want to be a lawyer."

This young man wasn't a problem. All he needed was to be reminded of his value.

"Your mind has to be like a bank vault," I told him. "You have to find a solution for every situation, then file it away so you can draw on it again. That's what lawyers do. Don't allow your mind to marinate on negativity. I understand your disappointment. But don't allow someone's lack of responsibility prevent you from realizing your dreams. On your way home tell yourself a story. Remember how blessed you are to be going to this school. Congratulate yourself on the discipline you have shown to compete in these classes. In those twenty minutes from the steps of Rice to the stairs of your home, add up the positives. Your mother is proud of the fact you were accepted at Rice. She sees a responsible young man able to walk home by himself and avoid any trouble along the way. That's who you are."

I saw him in the cafeteria a couple of months later. He couldn't wait to say hello.

"It's working," he said. "It's getting better. I love the way things are going now."

"Why is that?"

"I go straight home like I'm supposed to. I get my homework done like I'm supposed to. Everything is better."

All he changed was the perception of himself in the context of his life. Self-discipline cures a lot of ills.

The same could be said for being conscious of the decisions we make and the people we come across. It doesn't take a great deal of insight to appreciate the value of people passing through our lives. I could go down to the homeless shelter and feel just as comfortable talking to those guys as I do talking to senators on Capitol Hill, and I've done both. It's not much more than appreciating the fact that everyone doesn't function the same.

In the Marine Corps, we strip down young men and women mentally and psychologically so the fundamental values of character, honesty, and honor can be reintroduced. We don't renovate the building. We tear it down—and then rebuild according to values that one day might contribute to saving lives.

We know very quickly if somebody has a character flaw because freedom is restricted. Marines, particularly early in their training, have very little free time away from the unit. We don't allow people to maneuver around issues. You can't hide prejudice. You can't hide irresponsibility. You can't even hide financial irresponsibility. Our expectations are so high and so clear that we can see the slightest fraying of those values. It might not be a complete tear, but we know what's happening and we intervene.

A Marine isn't going to look the other way and say, "It's his life. He can do what he wants." No. Every Marine carries with him or herself the reputation of the entire Marine Corp.

The same is true of life outside the military, though it isn't always as easy to intervene. Leaders need to recognize that their example extends beyond the executive suite, the classroom, or even the home out into the community. That's why I am involved in mentoring the young men at Rice, as well as at All Hallows High School in the Bronx. Most kids are used to being told what they do wrong. It's just as important to remind them of what they are doing right.

Nurture their self-esteem, rather than judge.

8

Give Power to Your People: Don't Silo Authority

ONE OF THE MOST fundamental aspects of effective leadership is leveraging power by distributing it among your people. When power only flows in a straight line, there is never enough to go around.

Now, distributing power might be a foreign concept in many parts of the business and political world, but it's as fundamental as basic training in the military. The United States military is one of the few organizations in the world where leaders are graded on how well they train subordinates to take over the leaders' jobs. The Marines Corps, like any business, measures a leader's performance by the results they produce. It's just that the results are calculated in a different way.

In business, results are calculated by the dollars generated, quarter by quarter. It's a simplistic and often misleading way to rate success because the effects of poor leadership don't necessarily show up in a linear fashion from one quarter to the next. The full impact of decisions made based on short-term self-interest, rather than on the long-term health of the organization, may take a while to appear.

Look at the subprime mortgage market and financial institutions that have been forced to write off billions of dollars. For many of those companies the bad news has followed record earnings accompanied by substantial bonus payments to company officers. The problem, of course, is a systemic one. Those short-term decisions were driven by financial incentives often at odds with the stated goal of the corporation and the fiduciary responsibilities of its officers.

In the Marine Corps no such confusion can happen. A leader is defined by what both he and his unit produce together. One is never independent of the other.

You might be the smartest, most physically fit, squared-away Marine in the world, but your destiny is always tied to how well your subordinates perform. Most important, shortcuts are quickly revealed. In the Corps, cutting a corner might help you in the near term, but the system is designed to expose anyone whose personal approach is not aligned with that of the institution.

This concept of team leadership is fundamental to a military organization because the specter of war demands a sharing of power and knowledge. If one Marine goes down, the unit never falls apart because information is never in a silo.

Strong leaders empower others. And a good leader will never try to leverage his authority to get his subordinates to act. For instance, even when I was sergeant major to the Supreme Allied Command at NATO in 2003, I never used General Jones or his title to reinforce or otherwise ensure that orders I gave were carried out.

I've been in boardrooms and seen otherwise intelligent people feel the need to confirm a direction by invoking the CEO's name. To me that's a sign of weakness. If you prime the pump by telling those under you that a directive is really the boss's idea, not your own, they won't know whether you believe the command is right or not. By implying that you're simply following orders, you present yourself as someone lacking power of your own.

I've always taken pride in empowering my Marines. So when I became detachment (DET) commander of the U.S. embassy in Copenhagen in June 1979, I decided to put my deputy, Sergeant Pettis, in charge of the Marine House where the Marines live. This way I wouldn't have to take the time to deliver every order in person.

By virtue of my position, I was the one with all the authority. The question was whether or not I could distribute that power in a way that improved the chances of turning the unit's performance around. (It had a reputation for being lax). But it also meant that Sergeant Pettis would be overseeing other Marines who were the same rank as he. I had to find a way to secure his authority with the detachment, so I decided to have him cancel Field Day one week.

Now, every Thursday evening just about anywhere in the world the Marine Corps conducts what is called "Field Day." It's an arduous process of cleaning every square inch of the housing unit, which means taking everything out and scrubbing the room from the ceiling to the floor, from the windows to the door. Then everything is cleaned toothbrush style so it's cleaner than a hospital room. After every piece of furniture is placed back into the room, the procedure is inspected. Those rooms have to be immaculate.

Nobody likes Field Day, not even on embassy duty where housing is often quite comfortable. In Copenhagen, the United States embassy is a three-story, white building designed by American architects from MIT and the University of Chicago in 1954. With neither a wall nor a gate between the street and the front door, the structure nonetheless is secured by a highly trained Marine Corps detachment.

The Marine House is roughly three miles away in one of Copenhagen's finest neighborhoods. It is a large, luxurious house with every accoutrement.

I knew instinctively that if I called all of my Marines into my office and told everyone that Sergeant Pettis was now in charge, my words would have had little impact. Most people follow what they see, not what they hear. So I needed to use a different tactic instead.

"Sergeant Pettis, call your Marines together and tell them you are canceling Field Day on Thursday."

"But they are going to ask me what you are going to say, Gunny."

"You tell them it doesn't matter what I think. You run the house. Let them know you appreciate their hard work all week and that it is your decision. If the Gunny doesn't like it, then he can deal with you. That's what you tell them."

Pettis hadn't realized at first just how I was empowering him. But I knew that by this simple gesture, he would demonstrate that he had the authority to make things happen. And he would no longer have to worry about bowing to peer pressure.

If he had to turn around and validate this order with me, then the rest of the unit would assume they could circumvent him in the future, because he didn't really have any more power than they did. But by canceling Field Day seemingly on his own, he was able to make a firm statement that had impact.

"Hey guys, you did good this week. You kept the house immaculate. I know we're supposed to have Field Day, but that's not going to happen. And don't worry about it. I'll take the heat. You guys take the day off."

Later on Pettis told me that the Marines thought he was crazy. I knew they would. But I also knew that the next time my deputy told them it was time to work, they would work. They didn't have to hear it from me.

This kind of empowerment often is key to success in professional sports as well. Tony Dungy became the first African-American head coach to lead an NFL team to a Super Bowl title in 2007. Now, that wouldn't have happened if he hadn't empowered Peyton Manning to change plays at the line of scrimmage or adjust the game plan as the situation dictated.

But interestingly, when I arrived in Brussels as Sergeant Major of the Supreme Allied Forces at NATO under General Jones in July of 2003 and was charged with creating a sergeant major/NCO program at NATO, one of the early issues I faced was resistance to empowering subordinates. Since the European style is to manage from the top down, the idea of dispersing authority wasn't an easy sell despite the obvious benefits.

I needed to form a staff composed of people who were smarter than me, could go places I couldn't go, and do more than I could do. There were nineteen NATO countries involved when I arrived, twenty-six when I left in 2006. As you would expect, every country was unique in every way from culture and language to systems and operations. Some of those countries—Estonia and Slovakia, to name two—had been independent for ten years or less. I needed Europeans. I spoke one language well—English—and I had below-average communication skills in Danish.

Yolanda Terry, who had been part of protocol, became the center of my staff. Not only could she speak English and Dutch, she understood German and French and was fluent in NATO protocol. All I had to do was conduct the orchestra, spread the word, and keep tabs on our progress.

I very quickly understood the fact no one wanted to be told what to do by an American. I had to explain the value of the sergeant major/ NCO program rather than dictate the terms. At headquarters, I couldn't show even the slightest weakness because it was clear enough how hard the process was going to be. NATO needed to understand how to get the most value out of its 2.3 million men and women in uniform. If you only value officers and use the enlisted ranks as gofers or low-level worker bees, then that's not extracting full value.

The culture was one of control. No one wanted to cede control to anyone, much less an enlisted person. As a result many countries had lieutenants and captains doing what corporals and sergeants would be doing in the United States military. Eventually, and against extremely high odds, the sergeant major/NCO program was established throughout NATO.

The first time I was set to travel to one of the NATO countries, a male staffer selected the gift to be included in the gift exchange. He came into my office with the present simply dropped into a plain bag.

But when Yolanda got involved, she brought a whole other level of consideration and passion to something as simple as the gift exchange. She would brief me on the gift, show it to me, and five minutes later bring it into my office wrapped with ribbons. She showed a touch of class and a level of commitment I always found refreshing.

In the course of implementing this program, I went to every country to make an assessment of each situation. I had to be humble, open-minded, and listen carefully. I needed to explain how we treated enlisted men and women in the U.S. military, and why it was important to develop a sergeant major/NCO program across NATO to empower similarly ranked people.

Times had changed and the enlisted military personnel, particularly in European countries with mandatory service, were more educated than ever before. Many of them had attended university before doing their military duty.

"You have an intellectual advantage. Why put all the weight on your officers? You have ten smart people, but only one of them is allowed to think. You could be missing out on nine other great ideas."

I had to explain delicately how important it was for commanders to delegate responsibility for the good of the organization. Most of the people they would be disseminating power to were well educated, so they could be trained quickly and efficiently.

I believe that if you are afraid of delegating, you lack confidence in your ability to teach. Instead of holding on to certain responsibilities that were beneath their rank, these officers had to understand that this new program would ultimately help them to be more effective leaders. That's the message I took throughout Europe.

Now it was harder for some countries than others to loosen the grip on control. General Jones and I went to Afghanistan to meet with the Turkish head of the Afghan Security Forces. The Turkish sergeant major escorted us around the camp, telling us about the bunkers, the food courts, all the great things going on.

"Where is your office, Sergeant Major?" I asked.

"I don't have an office," he said. "I share one with the general's aide."

"Then how do you communicate with the other sergeants major, such as those in Italy, Norway, and Canada? Don't you have a place from where you can call them, inform them of what is expected, or reiterate the commander's intent? How do you do that?"

Here I had an opportunity to directly change the culture of the NCO of one NATO country. When the Turkish general sat down with General Jones and myself, he asked what I thought of his sergeant major.

"I didn't know you had one. He doesn't have an office in the building. Where I come from, it's important that my office is right outside General Jones's office so he can quickly and effectively communicate to me what he needs done. I noticed there are two well-decorated conference rooms on this floor, but only one of them is being used. To me it would seem appropriate to turn one of those into an office for your sergeant major. That way he will be able to pass along your intentions to the other sergeants major so you don't have to worry about the day-to-day welfare of the camp."

I could sense this Turkish general still wasn't comfortable with the idea of relinquishing authority. But with General Jones sitting in front of him, he said he was willing to give it a try. And he did.

Later, when we went back to Afghanistan, the general was so

pleased with the benefits that the idea made its way back to Turkey where the military started to assess how to implement an NCO program into their own armed forces.

Within four months of my arrival in Brussels, the program was up and running throughout NATO. It would not have been possible to create and implement a program of this size if I was the only one involved with promoting it. So we created and instructed mobile training teams that I sent out to various countries. These teams were made up of people from a variety of countries. When they would arrive in a country to explain the program, no one saw the idea as a U.S. model. They saw a model created by sergeants major of NATO for NATO.

By empowering these other individuals, I was spreading a new concept in nineteen different languages. It was an approach I learned early in my career and I applied often. And it was a principle that didn't stop for me when I left the office.

MY WIFE, RITA, AND I have always treated our daughter, Portia, as an individual. We provided guidance and established very clear boundaries for her when she was growing up, but we also consciously empowered her from a very young age.

It was a parenting model I learned at home in Hot Springs. My mother worked as many as three jobs, so my two older sisters, Ida and Ruby, were given the authority to run the house in her absence. My mother's authority remained in force even when she was at work. If Ida told us to stay in the yard, that's what we did because we knew she was speaking for our mother. If we had homework to do, or the kitchen needed to be cleaned, it didn't matter that the messages came from Ida or Ruby. They were the sergeants major to the commanding officer, my mother.

If they told us we could go to the store, then we didn't wait to clear it with my mother. So the idea of sharing responsibility, or empowering others to maintain control in the absence of the boss made sense to me, coming from such a large family.

If I had focused only on what other parents told me about how to raise my child, I would have been a decade removed from her generation. Instead I empowered myself so I could empower her. I had to meet her where she was so I could communicate effectively and effortlessly with her as she matured.

I read the books she read, listened to the music she listened to, and watched the television programs she watched. I didn't do those things because I enjoyed them independently of her. I did it so that we had common ground.

I noticed that she bought *Seventeen* magazine and *Cosmopolitan* every month. I knew she wasn't buying *Sports Illustrated* and the *Marine Corps Times* like I was, so I bought the magazines she read along with my own and took them to the office. To communicate effectively, I had to better understand the world she was in.

If she talked about Justin Timberlake or Shania Twain, then I wanted to be able to contribute to the conversation. I couldn't do that if I was stuck in my Perry Como world. I met her where she was so I could deliver those dinner table values in a way that she could receive them.

For whatever reason, and I'm not sure what it was, Portia loved President John F. Kennedy. She devoured books on JFK. She knew the names of his children, how they were related to all their cousins, uncles, and aunts in the Kennedy clan. When other kids her age had posters of musicians or teen actors in their rooms, Portia wanted a poster of President Kennedy.

Portia was in seventh grade during the 1992 presidential election year. Rita and I never talked to her about political parties because we wanted her to come to her own conclusions. We talked about people. Who is the best person to provide the most support for families? Which candidate cares most about the greater good of the nation versus narrow special interests? We talked about values. We worked hard to show her what those values looked like when they were applied to day-to-day life.

Personally, I never focused on party affiliation. I always looked for the right person for the country. Most of Portia's friends adopted their parents' ideas about Republicans, Democrats, or Independents. One day, I realized she had grasped her own version of our dinner table values.

"We had a voting exercise today in school. First we voted on the issues. Then we voted on the name of the candidate we liked. But the votes on the issues didn't match the votes for the candidates supporting those issues. I realized they weren't voting on what they believed. They were voting based on what their parents believed. I don't understand how you could support a candidate's position on the issues, but not support the candidate. You can't vote for a candidate if the issues don't match the name."

I was proud of her because she was speaking about what was important to her, not what was important to her parents.

To this day we don't always agree about political candidates. I don't rubber-stamp a candidate because of what that person says he or she will do for the United States military. They might move up on my list if their ideas enable the armed forces to better protect and serve the nation. But I'm not going to make that decision at the expense of feeding people who are hungry, providing health care to children without any, or watching out for people on the margins.

I'm looking for a leader who can run our nation like fathers and mothers run households all over America. They might have to borrow a little here and there, but most of them balance their budgets, provide housing, food, safety, and guidance to the young people in their care. They take those responsibilities seriously. They don't pay the electric bill then throw away the water bill.

⌐ ⌐ ⌐

LEADING THE YOUNG MEN and women in the Marine Corps has demanded the same kind of empowerment that Rita and I provided Portia. In a similar way, I bought an Xbox and learned about video games as part of my job. Young men whom I was in charge of leading grew up with video games. Gaming was an important element in their social lives, so I had to become conversant and comfortable with the Xbox, PlayStation, and the hit games.

Rather than pass judgment on those activities because they weren't a part of my childhood, or my daily entertainment, I learned about them so I could better lead.

Unfortunately, some people think the only way to lead is to be judgmental. I saw evidence of this when I was sergeant major of the 1st Marine Aircraft Wing in Okinawa, Japan, in 1996. I had stopped to watch the gunnery sergeant leading Marines through practice for a ceremonial parade later that day. Whenever a change in command takes place—in this case a new general replacing an outgoing one—a parade ceremony is held. I noticed that all the sergeants major were sitting in the reviewing stands in the center of the parade deck where all the senior officers and guests would sit later that day. Their Marines were executing the parade under the direction of the Wing Drill Master.

Every single sergeant major was complaining about one thing or another. One didn't like how the flag was being carried. Another didn't think the marching was synchronized. To another, the carriage weapons weren't aligned correctly. These Marines weren't being leaders, they were being critical commentators without adding anything positive to the process.

I asked them why they were complaining.

One by one they listed their problems.

So I said, "Okay, fine. Sergeant Major, you sound like an expert on the way colors should be carried. So you are in charge of fixing that. And you, Sergeant Major, you don't like the marching. You are now in charge of making sure the marching meets your expectations."

I went right down the line and divided the power among them. Now, each of them had the authority and responsibility to see that certain appropriate standards were met. So if there was a problem with the performance, they had to answer to one another

When power is kept in a silo, an entire organization can suffer.

DURING AN INTERNATIONAL CRISIS on my watch while I was DET commander at the embassy in Copenhagen, I realized I needed to engage my Marines on a more immediate level for their own safety. Once again my solution was to empower those under my command.

Early in the morning of November 4, 1979, as many as 500 students, known as Muslim Student Followers of the Imam's Line, participated in an attack on the U.S. embassy in Tehran. A female with metal cable cutters hidden in her chador broke open chains on the embassy gates. Although three diplomats escaped into nearby Canadian and Swedish embassies and another thirteen were released later in the month, fifty-two hostages were detained for 444 days until their release in January 1981.

Thirteen hostages, including women and African-Americans, were released less than three weeks after the takeover. They were flown to Denmark where an official from the State Department and I briefed them at the airport. We boarded the plane and explained what to expect when they returned home as well as what they could and could not say once they arrived.

Keep in mind we didn't have the Internet in those days, or cell phones. Windows software was still nearly four years off. The location of Marines on embassy duty during the crisis had to be monitored at all times via telephone. Even when they were off duty, they had to call and let the embassy know exactly where they were and provide a phone number where they could be reached at all times. If they left their girlfriend's house and went to the pizza parlor, they had to call and leave that number.

But instead of logging in every fifteen minutes as required, some Marines would wait until the shift was over and then write in all the fifteen-minute log-ins they failed to do earlier.

What would have happened if a bomb had gone off during that shift? How would we know where a Marine was? I needed to make these Marines aware of the possible safety consequences that came with failing to comply with the rules.

So I made every member of the detachment responsible for at least one aspect of training new members. If a new Marine came to join the detachment, he didn't get to speak to me for seven days. The rest of the detachment had to make sure he understood exactly what I expected. When he came into my office, his uniform had to be perfect, and he shouldn't have any questions about procedure or responsibility.

Now, when I evaluated the new Marine and if he performed poorly, I knew exactly who failed to do his job. It was the unit's responsibility. If that new Marine failed, then they all failed.

And that's a hallmark of the Marine Corps leadership training. To ensure leaders have the necessary time to focus on the most important issues, it's critically important to empower those they lead. It's also a way to diffuse conflicts born of ego, or in the case of the military, rank and tenure.

I DEALT WITH POWER and leadership issues again from the moment I became director of the Staff Noncommissioned Officer Academy in El Toro, California, in 1988. I was shortly thereafter named sergeant major in August 1989. The promotion to sergeant major represented a significant advancement for me. Instead of working in the command structure as one of many staff sergeants, I was now part of the senior leadership command. At the Staff NCO Academy, that meant I was in charge of all aspects of the program from managing and developing the curriculum to selecting and managing the administrative and instructor staffs.

I had advanced very quickly to that point, so I was in a kind of no-man's-land. Most of my peers were still fighting their way up the ladder while many of the leaders who mentored me were heading toward retirement.

I took over one of the most prestigious academies in the Marine Corps as a freshly minted sergeant major. I was also following in the footsteps of two great men, Sergeant Major Chuck Chamberlain, whose job I was taking, and Sergeant Major Carl Stucker. Those men were the previous directors of the academy and they left with stellar and well-earned reputations for excellence. Just to stir the sauce a little more, people there didn't like the idea of me being in charge. It wasn't as much personal as it was cultural. I was young and fresh.

I knew the situation. I remember thinking, *Am I capable of rising to the occasion? Will I be able to perform?*

I wouldn't have had any concern had I gone to a battalion with sergeants major of similar tenure. But now I was doing what commissioned officers did, creating and managing a staff. It's comparable to being a successful, low-level minor league manager, then taking over the New York Yankees in your first big league job. This wasn't a place for failure. I had to produce.

As director, I was charged with training, leading, and educating professional, noncommissioned officers in the art of leadership. Let's just say I wasn't accepted with open arms.

There were sergeants major senior to me who might have been given the nod. None of this was as easy as it might sound, despite my previous leadership experience. I was leading great Marines, leaders who had led their own units, squads, sections, and platoons. Some of them had done special duty assignment as drill instructors, recruiting, or been a DET commander at a U.S. embassy, which means they went through very challenging schools as well.

Now they were coming to my academy to have their leadership skills honed. There also were students who didn't have the same level of leadership training as the others. I had to take groups at both ends of the spectrum, pull them together, and make sure all of them came out the other side with the kind of quality leadership skills expected of all Marines.

If I couldn't do that, then they would not be able to go to the next level. Without successfully completing the Staff NCO Academy, they were not eligible for promotion. All of which meant I had to do my job.

The challenge wasn't limited to educating these Marines. I had to build a new staff of administrators and instructors. I inherited some of the administrative staff. But I had to find thoroughbreds, instructors who were the cream of the crop. They were gunnery or master sergeants, seasoned Marines.

I learned early on not to brand as my own the systems or processes I implemented. In other words, I never tried to make people do everything my way just because I could. I never wanted to build a structure that had a single personality. Then, when I left, the personality would leave, too, which would have meant I wasn't effective in establishing a system that worked independent of me.

I wanted to leave the program in better shape than it was when I arrived but flexible enough so a new leader could shape it to his needs.

I had to create systems and processes because I was following a great sergeant major with five or six years experience. I had to be careful in how I delivered my ideas and I had to be clever to make sure they were implemented correctly.

I couldn't dictate change. I had to build on what was already in place and let everyone know that's what we were doing. While I capitalized on my predecessor's great work, I never surrendered to the idea it couldn't be improved upon. Again, I couldn't do that by trying to sell McMichael's way.

People are willing to accept change if it's about making the organization better rather than making the individual at the top more appealing. I never approached them with ideas that suggested mine were better that those of the prior leader.

"We can't allow that legacy to suffer. With your intelligence, your brilliance as leaders, we can take it to another level."

Everybody knew the two previous leaders had been dynamic, highly accomplished men. They left the academy ready to compete for the position of Sergeant Major of the Marine Corps. The ink on my promotion warrant wasn't even dry when I took over. In fact, I had the rank and all the privileges, except a raise in pay.

As with any job, the older guys looked at the new guys and thought they hadn't been around long enough to know anything.

The young guys thought just the opposite, that the old guys had been around so long they didn't know anything.

I had to listen to both sides and find a way to fuse them together in a way that made the entire operation stronger. And I did.

Luckily I had experience with that mind-set. When I had become an instructor at Marine Security Guard School in 1981 I wasn't perceived to be good enough to be evaluated like the other instructors. They had tenure. I was every bit as intelligent, every bit as good, but they made sure I understood the culture.

To keep those ideas from festering at the NCO Academy, I had to diffuse them at the outset.

To do that, I partnered the older instructors with the younger ones. The infantry instructor oversaw everything that happened in the field. He was the duty expert on warfare. The duty expert on weapons was a rookie. So I paired the two so they could be more effective and eliminate the experience bias. They had to work together in harmony because those activities overlapped.

If a student couldn't read a map in the rain, or didn't know how to properly fire a weapon, the infantry instructor's job just became a whole lot harder. He had to rely on the weapons instructor or the map instructor.

Know your people. Know their capabilities and empower them based on those attributes.

As I've said many times, empowerment isn't a concept limited to any job description, industry, or age. Kids, for example, don't naturally assume anything is difficult or dangerous until we teach them that it is. When I see my grandson, Andrew, jumping off the couch or climbing up the stairs, I don't immediately respond by expressing fear for his safety. I know he's going to do those things. He's a little boy and that's what little boys do. Instead, I show him *how* to jump off the couch safely, and *how* to climb the stairs with one hand on the railing. I don't want to educate him about fear. I'd rather show him how to do things the right way so he can mitigate danger. I'm empowering him with that knowledge.

The other day Andrew and I walked for a mile and a half. He's not even three years old and I never carried him once. I don't push him; I give him the opportunity to make his own journey. Instead of telling him not to run because he might fall, I want him to understand how to run so he doesn't fall. He's going to fall whether he runs or walks. But I can't teach him to fear something from which he gets so much joy.

Everyone falls down. Leaders give us the knowledge and empower us so we can get back up again.

9

Expect Excellence:
Influence and Inspire

I WAS FIFTEEN DAYS INTO my thirty-second year in the Marine Corps on September 11, 2001. And only the fourteenth man to achieve the rank that came with my office inside the Pentagon. I had seen enough to know I hadn't seen it all.

I had grown up in a culture of excellence inspired first by great women at home and later by great men and women in the military. I knew what excellence looked like, how it felt, where the good separated from the great, and how world-class leadership operated up close.

What I knew more than anything, however, was that training and experience had prepared me for whatever would come my way.

In the United States military, the Marine Corps in particular, the expectation of excellence is more than a concept. It is a trait established, then embedded into the souls of young men and women by drill instructors and reinforced every day in every form by every leader they encounter.

I went through basic infantry training (BITS), the third and last phase of basic training, under Gunnery Sergeant Benny Ferragamo, who gave us a speech every morning about how to get through that day the Marine way. One of his favorites could have been a bumper sticker for the warriors he was working to create:

"Always be friendly, never get too familiar."

Gunny Ferragamo was one of those leaders who knew just the right moment and just the right words to make you reach down inside and find a little more. In that sense, military training by design is an evenly distributed mind-body experience. You need to be physically capable to do battle and simultaneously mentally tough enough to endure extreme stress that comes with combat. Gunny knew how to push the button that would keep us going even when another step seemed physically impossible. He had to. The South Vietnamese had invaded Laos in February of 1971, and as far as we knew BITS was our last stop before heading off to Vietnam.

"Remember what you went through at boot camp? Remember what you went through in Infantry Training Battalion? Remember what you went through yesterday in BITS? Think about what you are going to be asked to do tomorrow in Vietnam. You don't let your country down. You are a band of brothers. Those who came before you, the Devil Dogs, the Leathernecks, are the guys who have paved the way and left this legacy. Don't be the one to let them down."

He'd lead us out on what we call a "hump," a physically demanding hike through the hills that surrounded Camp Pendleton in Oceanside, California. We were in full battle gear with boots, weapons, canteens, and ammunition. The trails wind up and around the base, twisting higher and higher into the dirt hills. It was hot. We were tired. Our feet were blistered. The sun beat down on our helmets, not the nice, lightweight kind they have today, but those old pots you could make coffee in. That helmet bobbed around as the straps on our packs cut into our shoulders. All we were thinking was, "I have to pull this crap off and sit down."

Then, as if on cue, Gunny Ferragamo's voice boomed through the hills.

"Marines do this every day. The enemy doesn't give a damn about you getting tired. As a matter of fact, he wants you to get tired. He wants you to quit. Marines don't quit."

The words started burning into you. Gunny talked until chills went up and down your spine. Through it all you start to grow mentally, spiritually, and physically because each day it became easier as you settled into the concept that defines the process.

"Nothing is impossible. Nothing is beyond my ability to endure." I never lost my connection to those concepts. I wasn't the best Marine, not by any stretch of the imagination. There were a lot of Marines who were better than me, but no one worked harder mastering processes and producing results. Good isn't good enough when excellence takes only a step or two more.

By late summer 2001, the expectation of excellence had long become as much a part of my daily experience as taking a breath. Whatever I didn't learn about it before my current role, I saw practiced every day by great leaders like General Jones. I might not have witnessed everything the world had to offer in all its wonder—and horror—but I figured I had come pretty close to experiencing the full range of perfection in action.

On September 11, I was sitting in my office at the Pentagon giving an interview to a young writer. I had finished a morning workout and come into the office in much the same manner I did every day. It was a beautiful, crystal clear day in Washington, D.C., more like a summer day than one leading into fall. The young man conducting the interview had never been in the Pentagon before he was escorted up from security. We were still talking when we were interrupted and told a plane had crashed into the World Trade Center's North Tower at 8:46 A.M.

I turned on the television in my office, and we watched the images as we finished the interview. Then, seventeen minutes after the first crash, a second plane hit the South Tower. Suddenly the daily rhythm of the Pentagon building changed. People were beginning to move about, the atmosphere unsettled. By then everyone knew these were no accidents. Luckily, the writer had been escorted out by the time American Airlines Flight 77 slammed into the Pentagon at 9:37 A.M.

The building shook with an explosion that sounded unlike any bomb I had ever heard. The temperature inside rose, visibility decreased, people were nervous, some crying out for help, others crying for direction. Pandemonium.

On an ordinary day no one just wanders around the Pentagon. The building is so large—seventeen and a half miles of corridors—everyone figures out the most efficient way to reach his office and rarely deviates from that route. As a result, most people only know one way in and one way out of the building. Fortunately, my people knew the Pentagon unusually well because they had been there for a while, having worked for my predecessor, Sergeant Major Gary Lee.

The first sensation I felt was heat. Through the smoke I could see the fires. People were screaming, "Help him. Help her. She's pregnant. Help that elderly man." People began to emerge from the smoke bleeding, burned, their bodies blackened by the soot. One lady was so terrified, she simply collapsed. Then news spread that another plane was headed toward Washington. But as everyone knows now, before ever reaching its target, United Airlines Flight 93 crashed in southwest Pennsylvania at 10:03 A.M. after a heroic effort by passengers to regain control of the aircraft.

Security personnel tried to get everyone out and away from the Pentagon when word of the fourth plane came down. Marines are taught to head into the battle, not to run away from it. That's exactly what we did. But we weren't alone. Amid the horror of the day, I saw the beauty of the United States military. And I realized that for all the forms of excellence I had witnessed, the one revealed on that day was of a quality beyond even the most unreasonable expectation.

It wasn't just Marines, all the men and women of the armed forces reverted to their training to survive, protect, and support the nation. That was the essence of what I saw in those initial moments of chaos. They weren't concerned about themselves, only about what they could do for others. No one ran to the exits. No one ran for cover. No one looked for the media's bright lights.

For the average citizen with limited knowledge of the military leadership regimen, it might have appeared as if someone stepped out of the smoke and fire with a plan. Instead, it was the real-life execution of everything we all had been taught—commitment to service, an expectation of excellence, and the finest points of leadership—all of which had been imbedded in these people over their careers, long before a cowardly attack on innocent Americans.

When the time came to act, even amid the confusion of a crisis beyond anyone's experience, no one hesitated, there was not a moment of doubt. Not even the most senior military personnel in the Pentagon that day, many of whom had served in Desert Shield or Vietnam, had ever experienced an enemy attack on American soil. And yet their performance under extreme circumstances complicated by a multitude of factors, not the least of which was the possibility of another plane heading into the city, was nothing short of excellent.

Military training had prepared these men and women for that moment even though the idea was likely beyond their darkest thoughts. I saw people, some nearly burned alive, carried out through windows blackened and blown out. I saw Marines and others walking straight into the smoke and fire as if they were executing a mission that had been drawn up the day before.

No one looked for a medal, none thought himself a hero. This was leadership from deep within, executed with all the values, skills, and fortitude honed from the moment each Marine stepped off that bus in Parris Island or San Diego for basic training, to the reaches of leadership academies and Officer Candidate School, to the roles of authority they assumed throughout their military careers. Each person's performance was professional in a way that defied the trauma around them.

People talk about Rudy Giuliani rising to the occasion in New York City, organizing and establishing communication between the fire and police departments. Imagine every person, some of whom had only been around the military rather than a part of it, with the same spirit, the same focus, the same commitment to everyone in need every moment of that day. This wasn't a mayor organizing departments after the fact. These were people in the heat of the battle, displaying the same manner of calm and cool amid the smoke, flames, and rubble.

It was remarkable. To me, they stretched the idea of excellence beyond any definition of the word. I saw greatness penetrate the color and noise of a catastrophic event. No one could draw on past experience to know how it all would unfold. But their responses defied that reality.

The calmness displayed by the command and control elements, particularly General Jones, was exactly what I expected, though beyond most people's imagination. Within thirty minutes of the plane hitting the building, we started to bring order to the chaos. No fear, no worry, nothing but supreme confidence born of extreme preparation was evident.

A process to account for people, contact family members, organize busses to get our Marines and other military personnel out of the area before the state police shut down major arteries came together as if it had been choreographed and rehearsed many times. In the heat of the moment, General Jones emanated calm strength. He understood what had happened and explained what needed to be done, not only in the next few minutes but what would be necessary in the next few days, weeks, and months. He knew immediately that we couldn't rebuild the Pentagon that day, so he focused on the larger picture and what we had to do to get the country back on its feet.

America took a blow, and there was no break.

No one questioned the ability of anyone to execute exactly what he was asked to do. And no one doubted the fact each person would deliver. These leaders had diamonds embedded in them from years of training, decades of leading, and when it came time to show them off, the shine was brilliant. For the United States military it was a moment of absolute clarity. This country does not lie down no matter how hard it's hit.

If I had a video of what I saw—the response by Marines, the Navy, Army, and Air Force personnel in the Pentagon—I would run it in a continuous loop under the president's oath of office: "I do solemnly swear (or affirm) that I will faithfully execute the office of President of the United States, and will to the best of my ability, preserve, protect and defend the Constitution of the United States." That's all an enemy would need to see of America to know what would come next after another attack.

Everyone rose to the occasion. The day demanded not goodness but greatness, an excellence of an uncommon order. Never before had an enemy crossed an ocean and punched us in the mouth the way it did that day, a reality every one of us understood. Dirty hands, bloody fingers, burned arms, smoke-filled lungs, burning eyes, none of it mattered. Action. Performance. Excellence.

Not even in the grimmest moments did the attention to detail and dignity falter. We carried bodies out into the courtyard rather than out into the streets to limit, if only in the smallest way, the bitter bite of innocent Americans being seen lying dead. It's a day I have rarely talked about because the rehashing of those events brings back memories none of us should have.

When I made it back to my house late that night and Rita ran into my arms, it hit me. Neither she nor Portia knew where I was or what shape I was in. Rita had heard from the commandant's office, but it was hours before I walked into our house. My family in Arkansas called continually for updates. I had been consumed with my job, trying to bring some sanity to a day marked by insanity. All the while, they were home alone with their imaginations and fears.

In the days that followed, I received calls from sergeants major from all over the world. I felt the sense of camaraderie that comes with battle, the sense of connection for a common good, the good of the country, the good of the Marines Corps. Their voices were different, far different than when some of them called to congratulate me on being named sergeant major of the Marine Corps. The words came from another place deep inside them. I didn't just hear the difference, I could feel it, too.

We went back to work on September 12. Information had to be coordinated to eliminate, to whatever extent possible, rumor and confusion. Officers were provided armored vehicle service to and from work. General Jones volunteered his office at the Pentagon to the Navy leadership, whose offices were destroyed. Then he continued to travel to work and back home the same way he always had, without the armored car service.

One of the many examples of General Jones's insight and leadership became clear when the anthrax threat was first revealed at the Hart Office Building on October 15. Months before, he had ordered the Marine Corps' Chemical Biological Incident Response Force (CBIRF), which had been located at Camp Lejeune, North Carolina, to be moved into the Washington, D.C., area. When anthrax powder was found to have come from an envelope mailed to then Senate Majority Leader Tom Daschle, CBIRF, one of the few entities in the world prepared to handle the problem, was only a short distance away.

In the context of the time, a situation that might have been much worse was quickly brought under control. The notion of a biological or chemical attack was blunted quickly, though the threat once more shook the nerves of an entire country. Nothing gets done in the military without paper work, and we'll never know how many people might have been affected had CBIRF been forced to activate from North Carolina rather than Maryland.

THE EXECUTION OF THE wars in Afghanistan and Iraq were a consequence of everything that happened inside the Pentagon on September 11 and in the days that followed. By the time I went to Iraq for the first time in May of 2003 with General Michael Hagee—he had replaced General Jones as commandant of the Marine Corps in January 2003— I had been to Afghanistan to see the Marines in Task Force 58 take on the Taliban. Some of those same Marines, now seasoned warriors, had marched through the heart of Iraq just a matter of weeks prior.

Before we arrived on our May visit, President Bush announced on May 1 "the end of major combat operations" aboard a Navy aircraft carrier. The Marines, however, knew it was far from over. There was a clear understanding of what more had to be done, and the young Marines I encountered, their faces covered in mud created by sweat and dirt, the fatigue apparent in their eyes, were more than willing to do the job.

Our command team on that initial visit was very small, maybe ten to fifteen Marines. Every minute of a trip into a war zone is planned and coordinated with precision. These are highly classified trips, secured, organized, and executed by Marines. Nothing is left to chance. From the food served on the flight to the information provided regarding hydration, sleep, and security, no detail is too small to plan for. When we landed, Marines were there to meet us. They knew who was on the plane, which vehicle each person needed to board. The execution was efficient, professional, and without the slightest misstep.

For those of us on the trip, our trust and confidence in those Marines to get us from one place to another was absolute. We knew we were in a combat zone, but danger was the last thing on our minds because we knew the quality of the Marines in charge. If they told us to wear our helmets, we did. If they told us to grab our weapons, we did that, too. Fear had no place in our hearts because we knew the people in charge. We had trained some of them ourselves, and the Marine Corps had trained us all. Great leaders have confidence in those they command because of the quality of training they have undergone.

But what caught my eye even more was the level of execution. There wasn't a single stumble, not even a moment of indecision. The machine was well oiled and rolling. We moved fast and covered a lot of ground, much of it dangerous. I expected great performance on the part of my fellow Marines, but what I saw was flawless. On its best day, not even the National Football League's greatest team could hope to execute with similar precision.

As I talked to them, I saw their enthusiasm bubble out. They were tired, but not too fatigued to be focused. And they weren't tired from fighting. They were tired of an enemy treating Americans as something other than human beings and questioning the American way of life. They were just sick and tired.

I saw the real warrior spirit in those young men, some of them no more than eighteen or nineteen years old. Most had never seen combat before, but in less than two months they were veterans. I wasn't just proud that they had fought through the chaos that comes with this type of street-fought war. I was proud of them across the board—every Marine in every unit of every platoon.

I saw the warrior mentality that had been drilled into them from the first day of basic training. They didn't talk about needing food. They didn't talk about needing more water. They didn't want any more media coverage. All they wanted was the opportunity to do what

Marines are trained to do. And they weren't bashful about looking me, or General Hagee, directly in the eye and telling us that, either. It wasn't one Marine. It was every one of them from the lowest ranking Marine to the sergeants major and above. Even those who were previously inexperienced in combat had learned very quickly what it meant to expect excellence.

Some of the Marines I talked to on that first trip had been battle tested in the tactics of asymmetrical warfare in Afghanistan. But we train for every kind of enemy all the time. Our civilian counterparts sometimes think we prepare for war only when one breaks out. That would be like a taking the field to learn how to play football on game day. We prepare for multiple eventualities, and we are absolutely sure we have enough resources, training, and leadership to shift quickly and adjust to whatever the enemy does.

We might fight for a week straight but we are adjusting minute to minute and hour to hour. We have aircraft in the sky at all times telling us what's happening on the ground. We have systems in place to take out the tired or wounded and replace them with fresh Marines.

You can't do those things if settling for good is good enough.

Executing in what is often called the "fog of war" demands an absolute focus on excellence. And that is only possible if that kind of attention has been a part of every minute of training. I never saw those high standards drift in Iraq, even as the war became bloodier and more drawn out.

My last trip to Iraq, in the summer of 2007, was as a member of the Independent Commission on the Security Forces of Iraq under General Jones. Congress created the commission on May 25, 2007, and selected General Jones to chair a one-hundred-twenty-day study of the Iraqi military and police.

Though the country looked different, the Marines were exactly the same. Some of them had been in country two or three times over the previous four years. Their concerns were different from the Marines I saw in 2003. All they cared about then was getting back out into the field and engaging the enemy.

In 2007, many of the Marines were concerned about whether or not the people back home understood the difference between a good outcome and a great one. Would they be given enough time to accomplish the mission? Would they be pulled back before they could avenge the deaths of their comrades? No one was concerned about a schedule in 2003. Four years later, the calendar was on everyone's mind. The idea of leaving a job incomplete is antithetical to a Marine.

The issue of time wasn't the only difference. I saw satellite dishes on the sides of houses and on the tops of buildings. There was more vegetation, and the Tigris River, which looked as if it had been drained in 2003, had returned to its natural flow. Perhaps the most obvious change was the traffic. I had been to Iraq many times since 2003, but in 2007 many more cars were on the road. It made sense, of course, since there was little or no available fuel early in the war.

But the contradictions remained, too. Concern in the Green Zone was higher than it had been previously because a medical doctor had been killed by mortar fire a week before we arrived. People in the most heavily fortified place in the entire country understood that there was no safe haven even as cars crowded streets and brought traffic to a standstill. At the airport, runways had been repaired. The number of people out on the streets was dramatically higher, too. And yet concern over improvised explosive devices (IEDs), barely an issue in early 2003, was on the top of everyone's mind at every moment. In 2003, no high-ranking Iraqi government officials existed. In contrast, this time we had to talk to people in positions of power to fully distill the capabilities of the Iraqi security forces.

General Jones was selected to go because Congress knew the integrity of the information it would get—the unvarnished truth in a professionally executed report that left nothing to the imagination. We weren't going to park ourselves at one of Saddam's palaces inside the

Green Zone, wait for others to brief us so we could put it all in writing, and take the first plane home. We made our assessments by walking the country, talking to people, border to border, about every issue we were there to evaluate.

General Jones asked me to select a second sergeant major for the commission, and I was fortunate when Dwight Brown, who had been sergeant major at CENTCOM—United States Central Command—under Army General Tommy Franks, agreed to come along. Together with Sergeant Major Brown, we measured the morale of the security forces and the effectiveness of the training they were receiving.

Lt. General Martin Berndt, who commanded the TRAP mission that extracted a Navy pilot from behind enemy lines in Bosnia, had been in charge of all Marines in Europe. A TRAP mission involves coordinating the required aircraft and special and reconnaissance forces, and synchronizing the operation within a very narrow window. Lt. General Berndt was now charged with reviewing Iraqi border security. Admiral Gregory Johnson, who led the naval forces at NATO, evaluated the Iraqi Navy. Lt. General Gary McKissock came to review logistics. Others such as General John Abrams, who commanded the United States Army Training and Doctrine Command, came aboard.

Some of these men had previously led General Jones, and yet none of them balked at the prospect of reporting to him and heading into Iraq. These are great leaders, virtually all of them retired. Yet it wasn't enough to get qualified people to ask questions. General Jones put together an all-star team capable of asking the right questions. And then he inspired them by leading, as he always did, by example. We left no rock unturned.

The commission could not have functioned any other way. We were against a hard timetable that coincided with the September 10–11, 2007 "Report to Congress on the Situation in Iraq" prepared by General David Petraeus, Commander, Multi-National Force-Iraq. The political environment had become so toxic that some expected General Petraeus's report to simply mimic the administration's position on the war.

But I had been on the Hill with General Jones enough to know that no one on either side of the political aisle had any belief that he would deliver a report that sugarcoated anything. Whereas General Petraeus had only been in charge in Iraq since February 14, 2007, they had seen General Jones in action for years. They knew his leadership capabilities were such that being on the ground in Iraq at the same time that the world was watching General Petraeus wouldn't be a problem for either one of them.

It took impeccable skills, a fundamental commitment to excellence, and supreme trust in those he led to make an honest assessment without offending General Petraeus, Secretary of Defense Gates, or General Peter Pace, then chairman of the Joint Chiefs of Staff.

And General Jones did it all with an unwavering selflessness common to all great leaders. He allowed us to be the authority figures we are without defining himself as the star of the team. He wasn't there to make anyone look bad. He was there to make an honest assessment— could the Iraqi security forces, the military, and the police take over if the Americans left Iraq—and he made sure we never deviated from that mission.

We delivered our report to Congress the week before General Petraeus delivered his. It was thorough, honest, and to the point. But that's Jim Jones. He has done whatever his country has asked of him without ever taking a step back. When Secretary Condoleezza Rice named him special envoy for Middle East Security on November 28, 2007, she said, "I will look to him for candid, independent advice and assessment of our efforts."

IT'S THESE VERY STANDARDS of excellence and greatness that I try to instill in the young men at Rice High School in Harlem and All Hallows in the Bronx. By virtue of their presence at these two schools, these teens are on a path different from many others in their communities. If they have a mother and father at home, it's not uncommon for both parents to work at least one job. But most of these students go home to a single mother, who not only works a job or two, but also has managed to get her son into the school.

My job is to show these young men how to take opportunity and raise themselves from good to great in spite of the challenges all around them. I try to show them that greatness is attainable—it is not too far to reach. In fact, it's just a step away from being good.

I know what it's like to grow up in a home without a father. I know what it looks like to have a hard-working mother trying to maintain order at home while working multiple jobs. I've led men from neighborhoods just like theirs, and I've seen them rise above circumstance by making positive decisions and reaching higher than they ever thought possible.

So when I speak to those young men, I don't have to qualify or temper my expectations any more than Jim Jones does when he talks to Congress. My talks come from the heart wrapped in years of experience.

I explain the difference between settling for good when they are capable of being great. You make the Olympic team, that's good. You win a gold medal, that's wonderful. But if you can set an Olympic record, too, then strive for a world record. Don't settle. There's no harm in taking that step. As long as you don't back away from the challenge, it doesn't matter whether you are successful or not. Greatness is inherent. We just have to learn how to pull the curtain back, just like all those people did inside the Pentagon in 2001.

To make my point and to get their attention, I tell them I am HIV positive. At first, their eyes widen. Then I explain the concept.

"My HIV is not a virus," I said. "It's not a sickness. Instead, I have a positive attitude about honesty, intelligence, and vision. Honesty is based on self-discipline, self-motivation, and self-control. Intelligence is straightforward. Use what you are learning at Rice to enhance your knowledge base so you can better deal with life while more clearly recognizing how to take advantage of opportunities.

"Vision means never allowing yourself to be in the same place tomorrow as you are today. Surround yourself with positive, inspirational people. Rather than accept that the world is designed to make your life miserable, take the position that your life has been set up so you can take advantage of every moment. Avoid the negative ideas of those who do not share your vision. And when you are faced with a challenge to your vision, resist anything that resembles an excuse."

My message to these young men, and in my own life, is that good enough no longer is acceptable when excellence is the standard.

But it takes genuine leadership to transform the concept of greatness into a character trait.

10

Foster Functional Leadership:
Bring It All Together

I WENT BACK TO OKINAWA in June of 1994 to serve as sergeant major, senior enlisted leader, to one of the Marines Corps Seven Jewels, the 31st Marine Expeditionary Unit (MEU) Special Operations Capable. As I mentioned earlier, the seven MEUs are positioned around the globe and operate as fully integrated, though smaller versions of the Marine Corps.

My job was to make all the components—ground, sea, air, and logistics—work together seamlessly both on land and at sea aboard Navy ships. It demanded what I call "functional leadership"— the application of common sense, compassion, and logic to the fundamental leadership principles I had been taught over the two decades I had been in the Marine Corps.

As it turns out, I was both student and teacher in my first few months in Japan. I found out I wasn't the only one schooled in leadership skills.

When I received orders for Okinawa, Rita and I packed up our things for transport and boarded a flight to Japan. After flying for thirteen or fourteen hours, I went straight to my unit and got to work. Our furniture hadn't arrived and our housing wasn't even place, but I figured, *Rita's a big girl. She's been around the military for a long time. She'll figure it out.*

Think about that. I leave my wife and daughter in a foreign country with none of their things, no house, no car, and no idea of how to get around the island while I run off and set up my unit so I can make my mark in a new job.

Then I found out that we had four days to prepare for a four-month deployment.

To be "specials operations capable" meant the MEU had to be certified. That process included TRAP and NEO missions, which required great skill and coordination in order to execute them safely and effectively. Air Force fighter pilot Scott O'Grady, for example, was freed in Bosnia in June 1995 through a TRAP mission. Captain O'Grady was shot down on a direct hit to his F-16 while enforcing NATO's no-fly zone. He survived for six days behind enemy lines until the Marines came in and took him out by means of a highly coordinated rescue operation.

NEO missions involve the evacuation of United States embassies, which is not as easy as it might sound. We have very detailed plans, processes and systems to deal with virtually any eventuality all the way down to how pets are to be cared for and evacuated.

Marines in an MEU are many times the first into a United States military conflict. We were ready to deploy to North Korea in 1994 on my watch, for instance, if it had been necessary. We didn't know what the mission would be, actual combat or rescue, but North Korea was in our area of responsibility (AOR). And in 1994 the North Koreans had expelled investigators from the International Atomic Energy Agency (IAEA) and threatened to begin processing spent nuclear fuel, the first of many such threats. Former President Jimmy Carter convinced then President Clinton to send him to negotiate.

So the 31st MEU was on a seventy-two-hour watch, which meant it was ready to deploy at any time, when President Carter finally announced he had reached an agreement known as the "Agreed Framework" with North Korean President Kim II Sung. That's why any deployment of an MEU is serious business, even if it's a training exercise.

We deploy with all the weapons of war. It's all real, all the time because an MEU can be deployed anywhere at any time. Leading an MEU is a unique experience because it requires every leadership skill you have at your disposal. I had to set the tone with the sergeants major of all the units that make up the MEU.

Three elements made it challenging: First, every one of those components—command, aviation, logistics, and combat services—was in a different geographical area. Second, I had to tie them all together with the Navy so it all worked during deployment. Finally, we stopped in different countries, and that demanded intensive briefs on the local culture, habits, rules, and laws specific to each country.

We might be doing exercises with Thailand, Singapore, or South Korea. Everyone had to understand how to conduct themselves in those countries at all times, whether in port or off the ship on liberty.

It never happened in my time with the MEU, but good Marines can find themselves left behind in jail. An MEU can't wait. So I established a control system based on the chain of command. I brought in the unit leaders and laid out the rules. They were responsible for the Marines under their command.

"You will be walking the streets while those Marines are on liberty. You will be visible. I want them to see you on the street, in the bars, in the clubs."

It was about education. I wanted my Marines to understand that one moment of stupidity or lack of judgment was enough to undo everything they had done to that point in their careers. I didn't see any value in denying liberty and keeping everyone on the ship for four months. There was no need to make their lives miserable. I treated everyone like the adults they were until they proved to me they couldn't be treated that way.

We never lost a Marine on deployment, unlike the days when we trained in the Philippines, where it could be hard to maintain control. There was so much booze, so many beautiful women, and so much fun to be had that the Philippines had its own special lure. Some of these Marines were nineteen or twenty years old mixed in with older Marines who had been there and knew all the opportunities, good and bad.

I sat all of them down and talked about my expectations. I wanted to make sure the MEU commander's intent was understood.

"In every country we visit, do something that you feel comfortable telling your wife, children, or grandchildren about. Bring home an experience you can share with them. These are beautiful places. Don't leave Singapore, or any of these other countries, with only stories about the bars you went to, or the women you met."

I scripted at least part of their time by setting up tours to museums, zoos, and other cultural points of interest. I made the NCOs provide me with a list of the Marines who signed up for the tours. You could choose to avoid those tours, but then you had to deal with me.

There are so many moving parts in an MEU that functional leadership is essential. We had plans that allowed us to train to be warriors while making sure we qualified for certification when evaluators came aboard the ship. That can't happen if there is chaos in any one of the units.

Again, the elements of most MEUs are in the same geographic location. I didn't have day-to-day oversight of our ground forces, so I had to trust the sergeant major in California to get those Marines in shape. The aviation component was across town at what we call the First Marine Aircraft Wing (MAW). Combat services support was farther south on the island. In the case of artillery, some of it was on the island and some of it was not. I had to find ways to coordinate these pieces and fuse them together. Then, once we boarded the ship, we might have Navy Seals as well.

Before we deployed, however, I had to make sure we had security plans from the State Department in place. There had to be enough cooks to prepare the meals, enough people to clean up after the meals. I couldn't have a bunch of butchers, and no bakers. Every detail had to be aligned so the operation could proceed efficiently. I had to know we had enough beds, or racks, and figure out how and where we could do physical training.

When all those details were in place, I sat down with the master chief of the ship and made sure we created a brotherhood between the two services. The standard division—green side of the ship for the Marines, blue side for the sailors—wasn't optimal. Together with the master chief, we decided to eliminate separate lines for chow. We fed people when they were hungry, whoever they were. If we stayed segregated and failed to integrate, then whatever the Marines thought of the Navy and visa versa could be validated by the absence of direct experience. By mixing them up they were able to find out for themselves what the others were all about.

I also made sure the Marines exceeded the expectations of the Navy while we were on the ship. If the Navy wanted our areas cleaned at a particular time of the day, we made sure those areas were immaculate at all times of the day. We raised the bar and kept it raised.

That approach extended to every aspect of the MEU. I had a Marine who was in line for a promotion. He couldn't get promoted if he didn't have his Professional Military Education (PME) up-to-date. In his particular case, he needed to take a class, the schedule of which overlapped with a coming deployment. If he didn't take the class, then he not only wouldn't be promoted, but he couldn't be considered for promotion again for another year.

What was best for the organization, the Marine Corps, was to leave this Marine behind so he could complete his PME. That was the proper leadership decision because it was a decision based on the greater good. The Marine's immediate boss couldn't fathom going on deployment without his gunnery sergeant.

"I can't leave him behind," he said.

"Here's what makes us different," I responded. "You can't leave him behind because you might have to retrain someone else to fill that position. Rather than make sure that Marine fulfills the requirement that makes him eligible for promotion, you are focused on what makes your life easiest. Leaders bite the bullet, roll up their sleeves for the welfare of those they lead, so that every one of them is taken care of."

Rather than fight his intransigence, I created a diversion. We went to Colonel Mark Pizzo, the commanding officer, and explained the situation. I asked if the gunnery sergeant could attend an academy that started and ended prior to the deployment.

"No," said the captain. "He can't go."

I knew the Marine didn't have to attend that specific class at that time. He needed to attend the one that was scheduled to interfere with deployment. When the captain denied the Marine's ability to fulfill his PME in front of the colonel, I knew we had a better chance of getting that Marine into the appropriate class. The captain was more concerned about himself and how the gunnery sergeant's departure would affect him.

The next time I brought up the need for the gunnery sergeant to fulfill his PME, Colonel Pizzo sided with me.

There were at least three leadership lessons in that one small example. First, never choose self-interest over group interest. I knew that

Marine was solid and had the potential to become a great Marine. Why deny the Marine Corps the possibility of having another great leader?

Second, the captain didn't know his people. I did. It's essential for leaders to know their people's capabilities. If the captain had understood his people and what they could do, then he wouldn't have been so concerned with losing one Marine. Indeed, it forced him to provide an opportunity to another Marine who otherwise wouldn't have had one.

Third, Colonel Pizzo trusted me because he followed the first two rules. He always chose the greater good over the personal benefit and he knew his people. As it turned out, the decision was good for the MEU, good for the institution, and good for that Marine, who later was promoted on time.

As I SAID EARLIER, we deployed for four months just four days after Rita, Portia, and I landed in Okinawa. We didn't have e-mail or cell phones, so communication was extremely limited. The only time I spoke to Rita and Portia was by phone, and only when it was possible and I could afford to make the call. Though we communicated through letters, we never lost connection because of our faith in family and one another.

Still, General Jones referenced that first MEU deployment when I retired from the Marine Corps because of Rita's response to my sudden departure from Okinawa. When I returned to port, all the spouses, girlfriends, sons, and daughters of the Marines and their Navy counterparts were waiting for the ship to come in so they could take them home.

But when I walked off the ship, I was alone. No Rita, no Portia. No one was waiting to take me home.

"Do you want a ride, Sergeant Major?" one of the Marines asked.

"I don't even know where home is," I responded.

And I didn't. It was clear to me I had failed to practice what I preached: We should always maintain balance in our lives. If you put more emphasis on loving the Corps than you do loving your family, then you get to the top without anyone to share it with. I love the Marine Corps because it always allowed me to take care of the people I love the most, my family.

From Rita's perspective the message was clear. "You left me here to find a home, you should be able to find out where home is."

I hadn't taken the time to prepare them for my absence. Rita, however, knew all about functional leadership. She found a house, put it all together beautifully, enrolled Portia in school, bought a car, and found a job. It was a good lesson and it forced me to evaluate my priorities. I always took pride in my ability to walk out of the office as a Marine and come home to be a father and a husband.

Once I returned from that first deployment in Okinawa, I wondered, *Who's really the Marine? Who's really the tough guy?*

Rita was running the USO office in Okinawa, putting Portia on a bus at five-thirty or six o'clock in the morning so she could get to school on the other side of the island. Both of them were living in our new housing on the base, which was located on land that had been the site of a pig farm in the not-too-distant past.

I was out playing Marine, creating harmony on the ship, teambuilding, and focusing all those Marines on excellence. I came home to understand her trials and tribulations weren't any less than mine had been.

Rita showed me what functional leadership looked like outside the military. Her leadership skills allowed me to focus on applying mine to the MEU, which was unlike any previous leadership position. At OCS I trained officers to take care of our most precious resources, the Marines serving under them. Now I was leading seasoned Marines, some of those very officers I had trained at OCS, through certification processes and preparing them for battle. Everyone had to be at the top of their game because an MEU can be diverted to another part of the world at a moment's notice for anything from combat to a humanitarian mission. If an MEU had been launched to New Orleans after Katrina, I can guarantee you there wouldn't have been any of the confusion that developed between all the parties in charge on the ground.

Years later, Portia displayed those fundamental attributes—common sense, compassion, and logic—on at least two occasions while working for the Marine Corps, one of which involved assisting another MEU.

An MEU was dispatched to the Indian Ocean following the tsunami on December 26, 2004, and Portia, who was working for the Marine Corps in the area of combat uniforms and equipment, knew there were extra gloves in inventory designed to prevent the spread of disease and sickness. She had the foresight to know an MEU would be sent to the region, so she took the initiative and got those gloves to the Marines who needed them.

Not long after, she helped change an archaic rule that made Marines pay for any uniform alterations, even if the alterations became necessary due to injuries sustained fighting a war.

A sergeant, now an amputee as a result his war-fighting efforts in Iraq, was to be honored at the Marine Corps Birthday, which is celebrated every year throughout the month of November. He had to wear his dress blues to the ceremony. When Portia found out that Marine, who had given his arm in a fight on behalf of his country, now had to pay for his uniform to be altered, she took on the system. She could have gone along with the rules just as others had before her, but she knew it didn't pass the common sense test. The rule had been put in place decades before what we now know to be modern warfare with all its related technological and medical advances in the field.

By applying common sense and compassion to every situation, one is forced to consider the greater good over self-interest. I also find that approach produces results that extend beyond the unit and out into the larger institution.

That's why I took my ideas about functional leadership to the 1st Marine Aircraft Wing in 1995. Given my seniority on Okinawa and throughout the Marine Corps, I had a choice of duty stations after my time at the MEU. I decided on the Wing, which just happened to have a vacancy.

To say the least, it was not the duty station of choice for the gung-ho Marine. The majority of them wanted to go to the infantry. The way I looked at it, there was nothing anyone could tell me about the infantry that I didn't already know. Absolutely nothing. When you go on a hump, it's the same whether you are a private or a sergeant major—same distance, same location. When a private fires a gun, he doesn't do it any differently than the sergeant major does. They both pull the trigger exactly the same way.

Still, the majority of sergeants major aspire to roles within the infantry. When a sergeant major chooses Wing duty, the saying is, "take a Wing job and go with the flow." In other words, slide on through the duty.

My job was to figure out how I could become partners with the master gunnery sergeants. A master gunnery sergeant retires in the same occupational field he trained in twenty or thirty years before. He continues to rise in rank from supervisor to instructor and so on, but if he was trained as an aircraft mechanic, then that's what he continues to do until the day he retires from the Marine Corps. The master gunnery sergeant at a Wing is the duty expert and unit leader of aviation mechanics. Those Marines know their business inside and out.

I saw the Wing as a challenge and an opportunity. I didn't come up through aviation so I had no first-hand experience. By choosing that duty station I could learn about a unique part of the Marine Corps and in the process become better rounded. Most of those in my position didn't see it that way. They wanted to stay in the infantry. As sergeant major of the Wing, I didn't have a string of other first ser-geants reporting to me and providing all the information necessary to satisfy my curiosity like the sergeants major in the infantry.

Instead, I had master gunnery sergeants working with me. An avi-ation master gunny sergeant is bred to believe he is one of the hardest working people in the Marine Corps. He doesn't have the kind of sup-port structure that a sergeant major has. I saw that I could bring power and awareness to their hard work in a way that could be articulated and noticed throughout the Marine Corps.

I wasn't interested in coming in there as a superstar. I wanted them to know I was concerned about the welfare of those master gunnery sergeants and their people.

The first thing I did was set up a breakfast that gathered everyone in one place. Just calling all the master gunnery sergeants together was foreign enough to them because that's not what sergeant majors do. I focused them on team building, and socializing their work in a way that made them visible so they could build relationships with infantry Marines who had a different mind-set. If I was effective, then the in-fantry would no longer view the Wing with any less respect.

I needed a working knowledge of what these Marines did and what they faced every day. But I understood that they themselves are always better able to articulate what they need to make the unit work because they are the ones doing the job.

By creating an open atmosphere, they knew I was there to work with them rather than dictate my desires from above. I could have furthered the mythology of the sergeant major by staying out of the day-to-day fray, but I wanted them to understand we both worked for the commanding general. I didn't want to lead by rank. I wanted to inspire by example.

One way to do that was through honest dialogue. They needed to know I was more concerned about them and the organization than I was about myself. Most people in leadership positions are hung up on shining themselves so the top management notices them. They don't realize that the best and most effective way of accomplishing that goal is by focusing on and inspiring the people who form the foundation.

I wanted to make sure the Marines on the fixed-wing aircraft interacted with the Marines on the helicopter side, and that they all interacted with the ground support. I wanted them to know and understand one another and what each of them did on the day shifts and the night shifts. I worked out a system to take care of the night crew so they had adequate rest and time with their families. No one can perform if the expectations are unreasonable or the goals unattainable.

Rather than mandate physical training at 6:00 A.M., I sat down with the master gunnery sergeant and created a schedule. These Marines couldn't come off the night shift and then be expected to perform the next day like the guys who had slept all night.

I knew that if we could speak to their needs with dignity and respect, rather than authoritarian dictates that defied common sense, when it came time for reenlistment we had a better chance of retaining them.

If they had enough time with their families—and their families were cared for according to the promises we made—then there would be more support at home and better performance when they came back to their jobs.

I COULDN'T BANG MY head against the wall trying to figure out everything about aviation on my own. One of the first signs of stupidity is when you think you know so much that no one can tell you anything. Leaders can save a lot of headaches, man hours, and money just listening to those they lead.

The result was a shift in the relationship between the master gunnery sergeants and the Wing sergeant major.

By attacking the prevailing culture, I created the atmosphere for monumental change in performance. If I had simply changed processes and not the culture, then when I left the next person could come in and change it all back to the way it was before.

If you change the way people think, then their approach to those processes will take the organization upward and forward. I always focused on changing the culture before I worried about changing performance. That way the next person can change the processes, but he isn't going to change the performance.

I listened because I never forgot being in the shoes of those I led.

I had been a subordinate with good ideas that no one wanted to hear.

I knew what it was like to work twice as long and twice as hard just to get a superior's attention.

I never wanted to run a platoon the same way it had been done for a hundred years.

I always tried to find a way that would make my superior or his superior ask, "Who did that? How did he do that?"

Leadership goes directly to culture.

WHEN I WAS YOUNGER, I did whatever was asked of me exactly how they asked it to be done. I remember being told to swab the deck once. I thought it should be swept first. Instead of wasting my time discussing the issue, I went ahead and swept the floor before I swabbed it. The floor looked so much better when I finished that my superior wanted to know how I did it. I had influenced the culture. I had influenced change by doing something as small as improving the way the floor was swabbed. Common sense.

I also realized it was better to "socialize" ideas rather than present them as recommendations. The best outcome was to have your boss steal your idea and claim it as a product of his thoughts. Mission accomplished.

My approach at the Wing was no different than my approach at OCS or the MEU. I wanted to change the unit so it would be positively acknowledged and respected by the institution. The performance of those I led reflected positively on me, so the higher I could move them up the pecking order or the more visible I could make their efforts, the better.

But after a little over a year with the Wing, I had another decision to make in November 1996. Once again, I deviated from the norm and chose my own path. I decided to go back to Washington and work for Manpower Reserve Affairs for the same reason I had gone to the Wing. It presented a unique opportunity.

THERE WEREN'T MANY AFRICAN-AMERICAN sergeants major at Marine Corps headquarters in part because no one wanted to work out of an office in Washington, D.C. If I wanted to stay in operations, in what we called the fleet Marine Corps, then I would continue to carry out orders based on policies written at headquarters. I knew not all of those policies made sense in practice. The only way I could affect change was to get inside and figure out solutions rather than sit back and complain about "all those people in Washington."

By the time I left the Wing, Colonel Pizzo and Pete Osmon, now a brigadier general, were working at Manpower Reserve Affairs. In what would become a theme over the last ten years of my military career, I found myself in a job that didn't exist until I got there.

Lt. General Carol Mutter heard that General Osmon wanted me to work for him. Lt. General Mutter decided she needed a sergeant major even though the job didn't exist at Manpower, where she was in charge.

I didn't have a desk, computer, e-mail address, nothing. I knew there were people asking, "Why do we even need a sergeant major of Manpower?"

I had to be smart and diplomatic. I couldn't throw open the door and demand anything because I was the new man on the block. First, I had to empower myself with knowledge.

There were more than eighty Marine Corps programs at the time—everything from suicide prevention to housing, child welfare, life-long learning programs, exceptional family programs for those who had a disabled or special needs child, and on and on.

As with the Wing, the gung-ho Marine wanted no part of policy. But I wanted to become part of the rule-making process and see if there was something in the culture at the top of the institution that was being overlooked.

At the time, the Marine headquarters was in the Navy Annex across from the Pentagon and next to the Air Force Memorial. I realized very quickly the average Marine, even a sergeant major, knew the organization, but they didn't understand the institution.

Marines on the ground were absolutely ignorant as to how policies were created. I had learned everything there was to know about the *organization* of the Marine Corps. The idea of acquiring the same level of knowledge about the institution from a *policy* standpoint was intriguing from a leadership perspective. At the very least, I could contribute to new policies and directives that would have an immediate positive impact on current Marines, with the potential of affecting changes that would help Marines years later.

First, I had to learn a new language. There were so many acronyms being thrown around I needed a translator. I remember thinking, *Can I get a vowel with that?*

I knew some of the people at Manpower were just trying to let me know how little I understood. They were trying to shut me down.

Instead, they provided me with an opportunity to move ahead. I learned about every department and program. I took great pride in sitting down with the civilians who make up one-third of the United States Marine Corps, some of whom had been there twenty-five years or more, and talking to them about their jobs and programs. These were dedicated workers, and I had to respect their tenure and commitment.

When I saw an opportunity to make a change, I socialized the idea by talking to everyone who might have a hand in its implementation. By showing them I was interested enough in what they were doing by listening to them, they became more amenable to at least trying another approach. If they came to believe the change was their idea, then that was fine by me.

There were little victories along the way. For example, funding was going to be taken away from what we called "prior service recruiting." The recruiters talked to Marines who had left about coming back into service. The people cutting the funding didn't recognize the fact that the everyday recruiters often met their numbers thanks to the work of the prior service recruiters. No one made the connection. Once we looked into the numbers, I recognized the funding couldn't be eliminated without an inordinate impact on recruiting.

Taking care of the welfare of our Marines wasn't easy. At Manpower, issues were real-time events that affected people's lives moment to moment. Whether it was pay, healthcare, their children's education, their own education, promotions, housing, or hundreds of other concerns, Marines needed answers.

I had a situation arise with a sergeant major whose wife had terminal cancer. His time in the military was about up and he was heading toward retirement. Had he been forced to change his status from active duty to retired, the difference in benefits and health care for his wife could have devastated the family. Here was a man dealing with the death of his wife—the mother of his children—and after thirty years of service in the Marine Corps, he was faced with a situation that could destroy him financially.

A colonel at Headquarters Marine Corps denied the sergeant major's request to stay on active duty until his wife's medical issues were resolved. The rule says thirty years in the Marine Corps then it's time to go home. But the impact of applying that rule in a situation with those circumstances defied common sense to say nothing of basic human compassion. The sergeant major in question was one of my students at MSG School, and he no doubt knew he could come to me with the problem.

I went to Lt. General Mutter and explained what was happening in this man's life. "Under the circumstances, Lt. General Mutter, I do not believe we can deny this Marine's request. It is the right thing to do for this Marine and it is the right thing to do for the Marine Corps."

Lt. General Mutter listened, then she confronted the colonel in a professional manner about how leaders are charged with the welfare of those they lead.

"We don't have to do this, Colonel," she said. "We will keep him on active duty and take care of his family. That's what Marines do."

Rather than seeing a dedicated Marine leave with a bad taste in his mouth, we strengthened the entire institution by applying common sense and compassion. When I told him Lt. General Mutter had reversed the decision, I knew that sergeant major would never forget that the Marine Corps had been there when he needed it the most.

I knew the more I communicated with people, the better chance I had of influencing change. Sometimes it was simply a matter of looking at a problem from a different angle. Suicide prevention was another good example.

"I'm not interested in suicide," I told the head of that program. "I'm interested in prevention. I can't do anything about that Marine who commits suicide. I can only help his family after that. I want to help that Marine before he commits that act."

We took an approach in the Marine Corps different from the other services. We instituted a "2+2" concept designed to build cohesion between two Marines in a room together, rather than allowing them to be separate and alone. Then we instituted training and awareness programs that were carried on throughout the Marine Corps. Until then, the issue of suicide prevention was dealt with at basic training and never brought up again. We had made it a priority to put as much time and energy into investigating a suicide as necessary so we could explain fully and honestly to the family what happened. Why not put as much time into preventing suicide?

We knew there were signs of depression that could lead to trouble. Maybe a Marine had started to withdraw or he returned to his quarters and never left. We knew that despondent people sometimes suddenly start giving away items that had been extremely important to them.

We didn't need to change suicide prevention. We needed to transform the program so a drill instructor or an officer didn't have to wonder what he might have done differently to save a Marine's life.

Being at Manpower allowed me to give programs like that higher visibility so we could change the culture around that program. In the case of suicide prevention, I was concerned with how fast and how far we could take the education. Then I wanted to know how often the information could touch Marines and at what levels. But it didn't stop there. We also put systems in place to help families understand entitlements available to them upon the loss of a loved one in uniform. It wasn't enough to strengthen prevention. It was just as necessary to the support and aid the survivors. In the end, all those efforts led to a reduction in the incidence of suicides.

EDUCATION WAS ANOTHER ISSUE that didn't get the voice it needed. In 2000, I went to the Worldwide Education Symposium in Dallas, Texas. I was scheduled to speak, but I had become so frustrated with the previous speakers that I got out of my lane a little bit. Everyone had soft-pedaled around the real issues. They talked about what Marines needed and whether it was possible to get the proper funding. When it was my turn, I decided to speak the truth rather than sidestep it so no one's feelings would be hurt.

"We nickel-and-dime education. We are spending billions of dollars on the latest technology for jets, tanks, guns, and weapons, but we aren't educating the men and women who have to use that technology, fly those planes, maneuver those tanks, fire those guns, and use those weapons. Why bother spending the money on the world's most sophisticated war-fighting equipment if we aren't going to educate our people well enough to use it all?"

The place erupted. I have always believed the truth will set you free regardless of where and when it has to be told. I couldn't sleep at night if I bit my tongue and allowed poor decisions to prevail over common sense. With that said, there is a way to deliver the truth without being hostile or antagonistic.

We had a similar situation with health care when I was Sergeant Major of the Marine Corps. The Department of Defense had made progress by shrinking a large system into three regions, but we had done a poor job of creating remote locations where many Marines lived. I made that point to the surgeon general at a health care convention.

"You have to understand that these remote locations are hard to get service to," he said to me.

"Maybe I'm not as smart as you people here," I told him, "but I don't understand why it's too hard to get medical care to those people, when it wasn't too hard to get to those same remote locations when it came time to recruit those Marines.

"It seems to me if it's easy enough to drive there and sign them up, then it shouldn't be too hard to follow up on our commitment to service them with a health care system. Do we want their families to do without because it's too hard for us now, when it wasn't too difficult to sign them up to serve the nation?"

"Point well taken," the surgeon general responded.

Changes were made.

I ATTACKED OTHER PROBLEMS with the same tools—common sense and accountability. The Public Private Venture program between the military and civilian contractors was created to build military housing to civilian standards. Marines would be allowed to use housing benefits—the money they receive from the military to offset housing costs—to pay contractors in lieu of a mortgage. Everything with regard to the process was in place except the new housing. Why? It turns out Marine Corps housing comes under Navy jurisdiction.

"We have the funds, but we don't have the motivation to activate the program to meet the needs of these people. Meanwhile we allow these families to live in substandard, inadequate housing because the only solution we can come to is one that fits our desire to do nothing. The time has come to act."

When I finished, the individual in charge of the program told me he hadn't been chewed out to that degree since OCS.

More important, the authorizations and approvals needed to get the program moving were executed. I stayed deeply involved in the process, from coordinating with Navy headquarters to working with the Marine units and bases. Based on military construction money available, it would have taken eighty years to eliminate all the substandard housing on our bases. The Public Private Venture allowed the process to move much faster and more efficiently.

General Jones and I went to North Carolina, California, Hawaii, and elsewhere to cut ribbons and open the new housing. Suddenly, Marines and their families could look up and see the sky through a skylight rather than a hole in the roof. If something didn't work, then contractors had a limited amount of time to get to that house and fix the problem. These were real houses with fireplaces and garages, not antiquated trailers that could be found on many bases.

The furniture even fit, which was an upgrade in itself. It wasn't uncommon to get a promotion, buy new furniture, then find out it didn't fit in the nine-hundred- to twelve-hundred-square-foot "house" the military had provided.

A Marine would receive a pay increase with his promotion and want to buy nice things to show his family that he was moving up in rank and culture. Then he'd get orders and have to put the furniture in a storage shed behind his house or sell the furniture because it didn't meet the weight allowance for the move to his new destination.

No one wanted to talk about these things.

I did.

Functional leadership—common sense, compassion and logic—is the difference between ordering change and affecting transformation.

11

Find Your Compass:
Then Learn to Use It

THERE IS NO INSTITUTION on earth better than the United States
Marine Corps when it comes to training, educating, refining, and
producing leaders. Leadership principles are taught early and
often with an almost clinical analysis of integrity, character, honesty,
and commitment divined from the blood-and-guts tests meted out at
leadership academies from California to Quantico, Virginia and Okinawa, Japan.

The genius is in the system itself. Houdini couldn't escape the
never-ending wash cycles designed to constantly thin, slice, and separate the very, very good from the great. For those competing for a
space in the process, one of the secrets to success is to never forget the
road. For me, every duty station provided a unique set of circumstances; some by design, others by the ebb and flow of life outside of
the military.

I became comfortable with two facts very quickly. First, I knew I was different because less than 20 percent of the Marine Corps looked like me. Second, I got used to be the idea of being the first. I was the first African-American to occupy many of the positions I held. I also was named to positions that didn't exist for any Marine until I came along.

By the time I was named director of the Staff Non-Commissioned Officer Academy in 1988, all those lessons in leadership, the personal and professional, had become a part of me, saved and filed for future access. If my ascendance throughout the Marine Corps had been relatively linear to that point, the next phase represented a journey unique to me.

As a young sergeant major in charge of a prestigious academy, I had to know my Marines and make sure they knew one another. To build and then cement those relationships, I made sure we had social interaction on Friday nights. I wanted to create an environment where Randy Moss sat next to Tom Brady on a regular basis. It forced two sides of my team—the highly trained seasoned Marine instructors and their younger, rapidly rising brethren—to find middle ground.

The instructors became a band of brothers. We depended upon one another, not just professionally but personally. We enjoyed being together, and that bond couldn't be broken. We were turning out unequivocal first-class, top-notch students. I had been a part of that model and now I had to implement it at my academy.

I knew I was being watched. My superiors and even some of the senior instructors wanted to see if I was going to diminish the work of those great Marines who had come before me. Was I going to ride their wave and tread water, or was I going to take it all to another level?

The first thing I looked for was a way I could make an impact without diluting the respect for my predecessors. I did that by talking to those in my charge.

"This academy has been led by great Marines. Be proud of the history and live up to the legacy left by these legends. You didn't come here for yourself. You came here to keep this great institution moving forward with excellence."

I didn't have sense enough to be afraid of the uncertainties or expectations. I had been nurtured, mentored, and tutored by great Marines. Now it was my time to show them I had learned the lessons. I had to battle perception problems from those who had more tenure, but I knew I had support at the top. The mid-level Marines, who saw me as a peer, didn't think this kid knew anything. The older Marines, those who had taught me along the way, had no remorse.

"Leave the kid alone. Let him grow. He might be even better than you guys."

A LEADER SEES WHAT needs to be done and takes initiative. I always found that if I knew the rules and regulations and ordered change based on them, there was no fight. The Marines under me might not agree, but they didn't have a platform to argue from. Plus, they knew the bottom line was that I would always at least listen to them.

As I progressed up the ranks my responsibilities grew, so did my focus on the lives of the Marines I led. One time we had a young Marine, a woman, transferred into our command. She had worked for the secretary of the navy with an excellent record. She had been accused of shoplifting in a bizarre set of circumstances that nearly ruined her career. She was at the Marine Corps exchange with $200 to $300 worth of merchandise in her cart, a screaming baby and another child. She had been observed dropping a $15 or $20 pair of earrings into her purse as it hung on her shoulder. Now why would she be stealing something so cheap when she was spending so much money anyway? It didn't make any sense.

The issue had been adjudicated by the time she landed in the Wing. I read the report and I knew it didn't add up, but she had been punished. I was afraid she was being blackballed, so I started working to empower her so she could show her talents in front of the superiors. I couldn't focus on why she was there. I had to focus on what I could do to help her add value not only to the Wing, but to her career. I knew she had talent. She had traveled with the Secretary of the Navy and done all these wonderful things in Washington for the Marine Corps.

Eventually she worked for the commanding general and performed just as I thought she would. I was never going to eliminate the issue. That was going to forever hold her back. There had been people with the power to step into that situation and help back in Washington, but no one did. We nearly lost a wonderful, dedicated Marine with unquestionable pride and loyalty. She did get to retire, but not at the level she should have reached.

It's just like that dirty, messy $1 million in $100 bills. A little dirt doesn't change the value of the money any more than a mistake changed her value to the Marine Corps. The rules say you can't walk out of a store with something you didn't pay for. Common sense tells you to make sense of what happened. Dinner-table values tell you to use your heart before you open the rule book.

I applied those ideas to every aspect of my work at Manpower Reserve Affairs. As it turned out, Manpower became the perfect last stop before I was named the 14th Sergeant Major of the Marine Corps in 1999. I knew my platform.

I wanted to bring new ideas about quality of life, housing, medical care, education, pay and all the elements of military life that affect Marines and their families. I thought if we fixed those issues, then retention would take care of itself. Marines would be more comfortable heading into combat knowing their families were being cared for as promised.

I didn't want to give up any ground on war-fighting issues, but I wanted to raise the awareness in these other areas. Among other things,

I was able to work very closely with the Public Private Venture creating new housing for the Marines and the Navy because I knew from experience the living conditions were substandard at our installations.

I also implemented a program based on my long-held belief in empowering people from the bottom up. I started an NCO symposium that brought corporals and sergeants to Washington to meet with the Commandant and me. Representatives were sent from every command in the Marine Corps from Okinawa, to Hawaii and everywhere in between. Once again, not a thousand consultants could have told me what these people were able to convey.

I created a tracking system that allowed me to find out what was happening anywhere in the Marine Corps. I wasn't undermining the power of the first sergeants. Those corporals and sergeants were only telling me what their bosses had asked them to talk to me about.

At the same time, there were problems we encountered that could only be handled by strong leadership rooted in integrity. Two V-22 helicopters crashed and killed some very valuable Marines. The V-22, or Osprey, was designed to take off and land vertically with the long-range, high-speed performance of a turbo prop plane.

The media covered the crashes extensively focusing on the casualties and the cost of the program. General Jones dealt with the issues head on with honesty and clarity. He asked the secretary of defense to name an independent blue-ribbon panel to investigate the problems. People were relieved of their duties and a commander lost his post. It was a very difficult time, but General Jones displayed great leadership. He did the same thing on 9/11 when American flight 77 crashed into the Pentagon. The Secretary of the Navy's office was destroyed. General Jones gave up his office and moved to the Navy Annex so the Department of the Navy could continue to run smoothly. It was the right thing to do, though no one would have said a word had he chosen otherwise.

As Sergeant Major of the Marine Corps I had to do more than fire my weapon, run physical training, and wear my uniform properly. I had to step outside and meet the demands of the public. I carried the Marine Corps message to communities, organizations, schools, universities, and a variety of programs. Every year, at least once, I testified before Congress on the welfare of the Marines Corps. I called in every duty expert at Manpower, virtually all of whom I knew, to brief me on their program. They couldn't miss a point because in most cases I knew at least as much as they did.

General Jones took over as supreme allied commander of NATO January 17, 2003. I finished out my term as Sergeant Major of the Marine Corps, and joined General Jones at NATO in a familiar position.

Once again I was a man without a desk. There had never been a Sergeant Major of NATO from General Eisenhower to General Jones, but there will be one from now on because of the way General Jones went about the process. He empowered me to develop a professional non-commissioned officer corps throughout NATO, which we accomplished within months despite a culture of control.

We encountered the same control issues on our missions to Iraq. Those in charge there were so possessive of their power, however minimal, that they were incapable of delegating. The Iraqi commander in charge of transportation was the same guy monitoring the keys. It was like trying to move fifty cars out of a parking lot one automobile at a time. The Iraqis didn't understand the idea those jobs could be delegated and managed from afar.

Though we visited Iraq a number of times, the war was not under NATO command. The International Afghan Security Force (IASF), however, was. We traveled to Afghanistan every 90 days. Our visits were military and command related.

General Jones took the media, business leaders and others to meet with the various ministers of agriculture and finance, for example, to see how private business could assist. Joe Murphy, a former Marine and an extremely successful banker in New York, joined us on two of the trips. He was adamant about finding a way for farmers to grow money-making alternatives to the poppy fields. Joe could have stayed home with his family in the comfort of his success. Instead, he came to Afghanistan with a passion to make a difference. He went so far as to fund a feasibility study with the idea of creating crops capable of export.

There were no safe havens when we went to Iraq or Afghanistan. It wasn't like the Taliban or Al-Qaeda took a day off because General Jones and Al McMichael were in town. Every movement had risk and we never lost sight of that. When I was a kid working with Ross Rosborough's horses, we were taught to always keep a little fear in your heart because you really never knew what a horse might do. We had the right amount of fear in those war zones.

In Iraq we visited troops in Fallujah. We weren't just making a house call. We were there to let them know Americans might be against the war, but the nation has never wavered in terms of its support for the troops. We saw progress from one trip to another, satellite dishes popping up on top of houses near Baghdad for example, though it was clear there were going to disruptions throughout the country for a very long time.

In 2007, General Jones invited me to be part of the Independent Commission on the Security Forces of Iraq. The commission was chartered by the United State Congress and signed into law by President Bush on May 25, 2007. The mandate was to determine whether the Iraqi army and police would be capable of maintaining the territorial integrity of Iraq, deny safe havens to international terrorists, bring greater security to the country's 18 provinces, and bring an end to sectarian violence to achieve national reconciliation within 12 to 18 months.

In short, would the Iraqi forces would be capable of controlling the country in the event the United States no longer did. The question spoke to the beliefs stoked by politicians. If the war ended today, it would take years to remove all the people and equipment out of the region. Think of it this way: It's Memorial Day, Thanksgiving, and Christmas combined, and there are 500,000 people trying to board five airplanes with other people shooting at them. The magnitude of the operation is beyond the comprehension of the average person watching the war on television.

The commission traveled to Iraq in three groups, each spending at least a week traveling throughout the country. We visited hot spots, the Green Zone, Anbar province. We went north, south, up and down and all around Iraq. When the weather rolled in and made it impossible to travel by helicopter, we loaded into Humvees.

The report we presented to Congress September 6, 2007, was fair, honest, and to the point.

"The Iraqi armed forces—army, special forces, navy, and air force—are increasingly effective and are capable of assuming greater responsibility for the internal security of Iraq; and the Iraqi police are improving, but not at a rate sufficient to meet their essential security responsibilities . . . The Commission assesses that in the next 12 to 18 months there will be continued improvement in their readiness and capability, but not the ability to operate independently. Evidence indicates that the ISF (Iraqi Security Forces) will not be able to progress enough in the near term to secure Iraqi borders against conventional military and external threats."

THE UNIQUE COMBINATION OF these experiences has led me back to the future. In addition to continuing to work with the Young Marines Program, Veterans Affairs, various task forces, and doing speaking and consulting work for a wide variety of corporations and professional organizations, my focus has been on the development of future leaders inside and outside the United States military.

I have created The 4 DREW Foundation to assist children at risk. These are kids who have done everything society has asked of them only to be left with poor options when it comes time to advance. These are not disadvantaged kids—they are children at risk of having all their good deeds erased by a lack opportunity.

I've seen children, good kids with solid grades, no legal marks against them, from wonderful families, unable to continue the climb because their parents, both of whom have struggled and worked, make too much money, in many cases just marginally, for them to qualify for financial support. I don't understand how these kids, who have played by the rules of society and done everything asked of them, could be held back because they aren't "poor enough."

Their choices are to go to school and come out $50,000 to $100,000 in debt, attend a junior college close to home, or force their parents to change the very lifestyle that has helped nurture them. Rather than merely complain about the problem, I've focused on it. And I've created 4 DREW—Developing, Responsible, Educated, Winners—to do something about it.

We hone in on these children's natural born ability (NBA) while helping them create a network for life (NFL). Instead of forcing them to take a route that doesn't conform to their skills and interest, we provide scholarships and training designed to help them move ahead faster.

The 4 DREW Foundation matches children at risk with corporations who employ them in real jobs in the summer during their college years based on their talents.

At the same time, we help them develop a network for life by educating and counseling them on life skills such as nutrition, awareness of sexual assault, and how to protect against making life-changing decisions with negative consequences. By counseling them about the real world as they gain experience in real-world jobs, we are establishing the foundation for the growth and transformation of a well-educated young person into a world-class employee.

In the end, everyone wins. The student can follow his or her dream and earn a degree, the corporation or business that employs him during the summer has a well-rounded and uniquely qualified employee and society has a solid citizen. In return, we ask those young people to contribute their time and experience to the program as well.

I've seen what leadership can do to young men and women, some of whom have come to the Marine Corps from extremely challenging environments. I've seen bus loads of scared young boys turn into disciplined, confident young men in twelve weeks.

Not everyone has been lucky enough to get a head start at the dinner table at Helm Street all those years ago, and learn invaluable leadership lessons from Ida, Rosa, and all the other caring adults who influenced me in my youth.

But old-fashioned leadership never goes out of style. It appears that way only when it is in short supply.

Appendix
Make a Difference: Give Back

THE 4 DREW FOUNDATION is designed to provide scholarships to children at risk through the following principles:

Commitment: Inspire strong interpersonal skills, respect for education and a sense of hope through its Natural Born Ability (NBA) and Network For Life (NFL) concepts.

Responsibility: Empower youth to establish goals and then follow through on their commitments.

Possibility: Expand the perspective of children by making them aware of life's possibilities through education.

Support: Provide a caring, loving and inclusive learning environment.

For more information, please contact us at 4DREW.ORG.